The DEATH of Professional BOXING

Roger Yanez

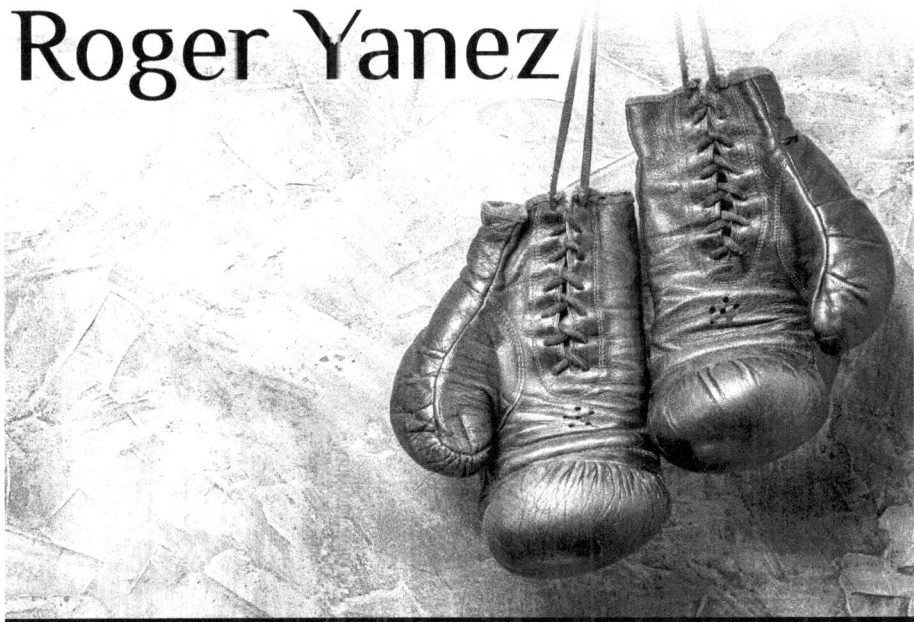

The DEATH
of Professional
BOXING

FIRST EDITION
Latino Book Publisher
Mesa, Arizona | 2016

FIRST EDITION

Book design by Yolie Hernandez
Cover photograph: BortN66/Shutterstock.com
Photographs are part of the author's personal collection,
except where noted.

The Death of Professional Boxing/Roger Yanez

xx, 126 pgs.

Latino Book Publisher
An imprint of the Hispanic Institute of Social Issues
PO Box 50553
Mesa, Arizona 85208-0028
(480) 646-9401 | hisi.org

ISBN 13: 978-1-936885-18-3

LATINO
Book Publisher
EDITORIAL Autores Latinos

I dedicate this book to my daughter Denise.
(Pictured with the Phoenix Suns Gorilla)

TABLE OF CONTENTS

FOREWORD

I have been an avid sports fan of boxing, baseball, football, basketball and soccer. Among these sports, boxing used to be my favorite. Growing up in the Olivas household, I recall the many TV boxing matches and of course, the Gillett Cavalcade of Sports which featured boxing. I have fond memories of my Dad, along with relatives and neighbors coming over to our house to watch the boxing matches that were offered via television. Wow, what an era of boxing skills and punches!

Attending and following the sport of boxing for the past sixty-years has been one of my interests. However, over the past ten years, I have rapidly been losing interest and after reading the introduction of this book offered by an expert boxer and seasoned boxing referee, Roger Yanez, I now understand why this sport is dying.

Sports fans love to attend events or watch key sporting events on television. When the sport becomes non-competitive, boring and non-combative as witnessed by the most recent Mayweather and Pacquiao Mega-Fight in Las Vegas, Nevada, fans become not only disappointed, but also begin to question the sport and their investment in time and money. Why pay for boxing tickets or even waste your time viewing a boxing match when two boxers run and hide or just tap each other instead of going "toe-to-toe." The obvious winners in the Mayweather/Pacquiao fights are the boxers promoters and the pay-per-view TV industry!

Boxing is now at a cross roads, either this sport now begins its demise or re-invents itself and offers fans a more exciting, creative and combative venue. Roger Yanez offers some strong rationale on how the sport of boxing will someday be in the annals of history as a former sport that came to an end. He also offers some exciting and creative solutions on how boxing can be rejuvenated and offer fans the opportunity to cheer for their champion in a highly synchronized scoring announcement after each round. In addition, the idea of the winner collecting his millions only when the true champion is crowned, with the loser forfeiting his purse is truly a revolutionary way to add creative juices to the sport of boxing. Further, as Roger states, promoters and boxers should pay a steep fine or be incarcerated for cheating the fans if boxers do not stand "toe-to-toe." It's not about the match or boxers, it's about the fans.

Promoters and boxers, should learn from other rejuvenated sports that have made a turnaround like basketball, baseball, soccer and football: you cannot survive without immediate and revolutionary changes to the sport and of course, without fans! Just like the movie, "*Field of Dreams,*" their famous quote: build it and they will come.

Louis Olivas, Ed.D.
Professor Emeritus
Arizona State University

PROLOGUE

For the past 100 years, the sport of boxing has existed in a static, mental, frozen zone, oblivious to the excitement that entertains the people. These folks, the sports fans, spend millions of dollars every day of the week looking for the magic that occurs in the entertainment business, but they have excluded the sport of boxing as an avenue. Once a year these folks gather to watch one so-called big fight. Albert Einstein is credited for stating that to do the same thing over and over again, expecting to see change, is not very smart; he calls it idiocy.

Most professional athletes are wealthy, and many earn two-million bucks a year, with the exception of professional boxers, due to the fact that they have to earn a living to support their hobby. This book is the path that leads to affluence for all of the gladiators. That path will materialize when the sport of professional boxing moves half of the basketball, football and baseball fans into the boxing arena. When the boxing raids the number of major sports fans, the fighters will earn enough money so that they will not have to work for a living, and therein, will be able to train eight hours a day. When that occurs, title boxing champions will also become wealthy.

Success in that endeavor will become apparent when we implement three minor administrative changes: the method of open scoring, (announcing the official score at the end of each round); the system in which the warriors earn their prize; and, expanding a paragraph in the boxing rules to broaden the definition of the word *foul*. The chapter on open scoring in this book proves that this method works, and the other two changes are necessary common-sense changes.

Today both fighters of a boxing match sign a contract which states that they *will* fight in every round, and at the end of the show both will get paid, regardless of the outcome of the fight, even if they both dance all night. When two warriors know that the purse is the same, why get hurt? The history of many mega title fights shows that matches have ended with no trauma to the face of the contenders because they just performed in a show; they duped the fans, and that's okay in professional boxing. In the entertainment industry, such as in professional wrestling, the fiduciaries are not in conflict with the show, but in professional boxing the fiduciaries are, indeed, in conflict; but no one has noticed. In all professional competitive endeavors the outcome is the big trophy or the monies, where wagering is a big way of life. The element or potential of collusion then becomes a very serious matter. A few of those who suspect that "something is rotten in Denmark" rationalize—for those involved—that they are only good-businessmen.

In all professional sports, it's criminal for one to be aware of the outcome before the end of that show, because a few of the fans wager on the outcome. If fake boxing occurs, someone is always aware of the outcome of that battle, therefore that element of collusion must be removed or addressed. All contracts must show that the person who is victorious shall receive an additional fifty percent in pay. In a big fight that includes a guaranteed purse, for one of the warriors, that purse shall be honored when he is victorious; if he loses the match, his opponent will get the purse. At the end of a world-title bout where an ambulance is not needed for both fighters, we have a situation in which something is wrong, and the commission should put someone in jail.

A fourth change I propose is to state that the size of the boxing ring shall *not* be larger than 14 feet square. Additionally, that when the revenues of the promotion exceed $70,000, all of the rules, as outlined in Title 4 Chapter 3 of the Arizona Revised Status, shall be enforced to the letter of the law. Regarding the proposed change in the rules, I will explain how it will contribute to bringing back the boxing fan to the arenas in great numbers.

In the May 2015 issue of The Ring magazine, one of their writers clearly outlines the plan and names of the next per-annual fix the fight clan: I win the first fight, you win the second fight, and we all win in the third fight. And Las Vegas is the scapegoat because this occurrence happens just once a year. If the proposed changes that I outline in *The Death of Professional Boxing* are implemented, Las Vegas will be able to host one or two big fights... per month.

This book was first conceived on May 3, 2015, the day after Manny Pacquiao sacrificed the Philippine people for money. This happened when he fought Floyd Mayweather, Jr. Sometimes plans do not work exactly as intended, however, the third fight generally occurs. Which means that their second fight shall occur in the near future. In the meantime, a different fight of the same clan is in progress. On April 9, 2016 we saw the third fight between Manny Pacquiao and Tim Bradley at the *MGM* Grand *Las Vegas* Hotel & Casino. In most of these fights, none of the gladiators would be considered for an academy award, because most of the officials that have been in the ring, several hundred times, can't be fooled by a punch that is pulled.

INTRODUCTION

In the last century, the sport of boxing has not witnessed *one single* change because the powers that be were held hostage by a political system that fears negative publicity.

The mega-fights in Las Vegas, Nevada—where most of the best boxing matches take place—have been a dance contest for a long time. As a result, "The Gambling Capital of the World" is losing large amounts of money because half of the fans exit the casinos after a fight feeling *very angry*; and angry customers do not spend money.

If you don't get it, I'll explain it to you all. There are several reasons for this dilemma: We don't pay the gladiators to fight; we pay them to just show-up. Before the fight, all professional boxers sign an agreement stating that they *will fight*; it's the law. If a boxer fails to fight, it's a foul. However, regardless of whether they fight or not, they still get paid at the end of the show. To make matters worse, both gladiators in a match know the amount they will be paid, and they both get the same amount. Now, do you get it? No! In most competitive endeavors only one trophy is awarded, and the loser gets *nada*, or receives less than the contestant who is victorious.

Today, the typical fight scenario that gives the appearance that something is not right is a boxing match where the best, meanest and fastest gladiators in the world emerge from a 12 round battle *without* a mark or scar on their face. This type of scenario indicates that they faked their first two fights, which then guarantees them a third make-believe fight. The guaranteed purse is fine, but only if he is victorious. If a boxer loses the fight the purse *must* go to his opponent, and then the loser gets a lesser amount. When boxers exchange real *chingazos* (blows), everybody is happy—maybe a little exhausted—but still happy. When the fight fiduciaries in Las Vegas make changes, we will see a mega-fight once a week in a casino that has two ambulances ready and waiting for the gladiators at the end of their performance.

The fight statistics—a worthless appendage—are finally showing its real purpose: they count the activities of both contestants when they are at their best and their performance during a mega-battle. These statistics reveal that former champions usually threw between 600 and 1,000 punches during a ten rounder. For instance, the statistics for the May 2, 2015 match between Floyd Mayweather, Jr. versus Manny Pacquiao—billed as "The Fight of the Century"—shows the following numbers:

	Punches	Landed	Missed
Mayweather	435	148	66%
Pacquiao	429	81	81%

Mayweather won the fight by a unanimous decision and reportedly earned somewhere between $220 and $230 million, while Pacquiao, the loser, received around $100 million. Writing about the fight between the American and Filipino boxers, Nancy Armour, columnist for USA TODAY Sports, called it "The Farce of the Century." Ten-time World Champion Oscar de la Hoya did the same thing several times. My friend Guero called it a dull fight. *Greed* clouds the brain into thinking that the boxing fans can be duped.

The statistics for the September 14, 2013 fight between Mayweather and Mexican boxer Saul "Canelo" Alvarez are equally impressive.

Canelo's trainer expected to see 2,000 punches from his boxer. Canelo actually threw a total of 526 punches, and landed only 117. Alvarez was guaranteed $5 million. He got wealthy, so why get hurt? Professional wrestling, in comparison, is more exciting than the last ten boxing mega-fights in Las Vegas.

As a professional boxing referee, I worked approximately 3,110 fights, and I never tolerated disrespect for the boxing fans. If I had been working the Mayweather/Pacquiao fight, I would have stopped the battle during the second round, called both warriors and their trainers to the center of the ring, and forewarned them regarding a fake fight. If the match did not improve after my warning, I would have then stopped the contest, and then ask the Boxing Commission to call the police and put both fighters and their trainers in jail.

Two minor changes to the rules and to the laws will change that sad scenario: "The one that is victorious in the match shall receive twice as much as the loser of that match." And add to the rule book in the foul section: "Any action or movement that could not lead to mayhem, such as running, dancing and holding is a foul." And this shall not be tolerated by the referee in charge. Additionally, the commission *shall* approve the boxer's payroll.

The words health and safety are paramount in boxing. However, they are not in professional football because boxing does not have the fan base that football does, regardless of the fact that football is one of the most dangerous sports, while boxing is one of the safest. The element of brutality is ignored in all the sports that have a huge fan base. Therein the athletes become wealthy. In football the average salary of players is $2 million dollars a year, according to Forbes.

So the handwriting is on the wall. Stop parroting the word "safety" and allow the trainer and the owners of the fighters to worry about the health of their boxers. The trainer is the only person who knows of existing physical or mental conditions that could surface during a battle. Therefore, the rules should give them the authority to throw in the towel when they want to stop a fight. At this juncture, the ring physician may be summoned by the referee.

BOXING IN THE MID-1960S

Boxing almost perished around 1965. The sport did not die because we are dumb. I am certain that there are a few intelligent people in the business of boxing. Maybe because we don't understand the meaning of the word *transparency or openness*, or maybe there are some other obvious reasons for our demise.

On December 10, 1965 a fight was seen on color television for the first time. Thus, television revived the sport of boxing and supported it until about 2007... when they left town. Since then, broadcasts have used professional boxing as fill-ins, between other professional sporting events. In appreciation for what they did for boxing we have ignored the value of the TV commercial. At every fight that goes the distance, it takes officials an average of five minutes to tally the score card. We are oblivious of the fact that the short commercial is worth $100 grand, and that most recent fight commercials were worth $4.5 million.

In boxing we treat the fans as if they are stupid. "They are too dumb to be able to keep score of a fight," is a common assumption. For keeping the score of a fight we use a boxing judge, one who possesses an innate, magical, and secret ability to score the fights. At the end of a match that goes the distance, the mindless uncertainness of the outcome of the fight forces the fans to exit the arena upset and angry. For example, in the sport of golf, a very huge number of paying fans show up for four consecutive days, from sun-up to sun-down, to watch golfers chase a tiny ball that no one can see. Ladies wearing high-heeled shoes watch players walk by, on the way to a small patch of grass, pushing a ball that they can't see because it's too small. Employees are paid to walk around in the crowds telling them when to cheer. I believe that everybody in boxing should go watch the golfers because we are too dumb; we don't know anything about business psychology and the behavior patterns of crowds.

A recent issue of The Ring—the legendary American boxing magazine that has been published since 1922—shows that in the top-ten of their fighter ratings, 17 percent of boxers are from the U.S., and 20 percent are from Mexico. This proves that boxing is an international—in fact a world-wide sport. Therefore, the entire boxing world has to share the blame for the death of professional boxing because they all keep score in the same fashion: hiding the score from the fans.

In 2011, Arizona politicians noticed that Ultimate Fighting Championship (UFC) gladiators were beginning to make a great amount of money, and that the sport had the potential of becoming a good source of revenues for the State government, so they asked the Boxing Commission for their help. The response from the commission was a sure negative. Bare-knuckle bouts would never be sanctioned by Arizona, nor in any other State... The Arizona Legislature passed it anyway.

Due to the mentality of the Boxing Commission, a myth has strangled the political-system into believing that they had ostracized the UFC, by cleaning it up. They legitimized the new sport by calling it something else. They added the words Mixed Martial Arts to the Boxing Commission title. The commission did not realize that the two sports are identical, and that the only difference is the appearance of the venue. Instead of using a rope to establish the boundary of the platform, thus sensationalizing the sport, they use a chain-linked fence that requires heavy posts that hold up the fence, and the added weight of the platform requires a stronger ring structural design.

The objective of a boxing match is to render an opponent mentally or physically incapacitated. This objective is accomplished, exclusively, by administering mayhem while wearing boxing gloves. A few rules regulate the UFC endeavor: No striking the groin and only the front of the opponent's body. The UFC gladiators should not have to be told that they must protect themselves, at all times, while in the ring but they are told that anyway. The rules also state that hitting behind the head or on the kidneys is forbidden, which means that if by some accident your opponent exposes his back you can't strike him. In this sport, the warrior who is a war-machine usually prevails. The action is so fast that occasionally the back is exposed and, therefore, a fighter gets walloped in the back, and then someone gets reprimanded.

The word bare-knuckle fighting connotes something brutal and barbaric and therefore not allowed in a civilized world. The simple truth is that bare-knuckle fighting *does not* exist. Let me say it again: bare-knuckle fighting has never existed. If a fist were to hit a head that's harder than wood, the knuckle would shatter. An internet definition describes the knuckle and fist as a highly-complex assortment of very essential and a delicate part of the human anatomy. It has 27 small bones and ligaments that can be used to form an obscene gesture. If that fist is not protected, permanent injuries could result to it, and the owner could become disabled. Without the hand and wrist one would be unable to use toilet paper. If you still don't get it, a leather or a boxing-glove is for the protection of the hand, not for the protection of your opponent.

BOXING AND THE UFC

All professional athletes are wealthy with the exception of boxers. They are wealthy because they are in the entertainment business. The boxer needs an eight-hour job to pay rent and put food on the table. Boxing is a hobby for evenings and weekends. Therefore, we must introduce reform that will enable the gladiator to train instead of working for a living.

The fan shows up in the nosebleed section (the highest and farthest from the activity) from where they need to use binoculars or telephoto equipment that enables them to watch the action. However, they don't use that equipment; why not? Very simple: since they can't see the action it must be the *score* which excites them. In a boxing match, during the rest period, between rounds, fans socialize and indulge in their favorite beverages. In a match that goes the distance the decision is always a mystery, and when the decision is announced half of the fans are always completely dumbfounded, flabbergasted and angry. Who needs that aggravation? Let's go to a sport where we always know why the score is what it is. Most of the fans know what fisticuffs is all about, and they understand the rules. Therefore, in a full bout without any of the contestants being knocked out, we need to eliminate the element of collusion that exists, when the ring judges are out adding their scoring cards.

The recommended change is a simple business administrative change, a change that will revolutionize the proceeds at the gate, which in an open scoring period in 1967 increased the gate 500 percent in only three shows. Sports fans watch boxing as a form of entertainment and they call it a sport. However, boxing is not a sport to the gladiators. Picture yourself in the ring with a "gorilla" that is trying to knock your head off. And if that's not enough, imagine that all of your friends and relatives are watching the contest. Is it a sport especially when your hide is the prize?

The UFC has replaced professional boxing because most of their battles do not go the distance; they end in a knockout. A lot of the action occurs while on the canvas. Anything is fair in those fights: kicking, hitting anywhere, and a glove may be used to protect the hands. Not allowed are eye-gouging, biting, and hitting below the belt. Wrestlers do not need a cage: the chain-linked fence is for drama, and protects the fans from imaginary wild bulls. In fights that go the distance, the UFC still hides the score the same way as they do in boxing. When they finally wise-up and go to open scoring, their fan base will skyrocket.

Therefore, I offer three minor administrative changes that will, overnight, revolutionize the gate receipts. In Chapter 8 of this book, I talk about the history of the open scoring system that was used in 1967. At that time, this system was also approved by the Arizona Boxing Commission. While in use, the gate climbed from 300 to 1,700 fans in only three shows. The changes I propose are:

1. Announce the official score at the end of each round.

2. All contracts that guarantee the amount of the purse shall be honored *when* a boxer is victorious. If he loses the battle, his opponent will obtain the guarantee.

3. Expanding a paragraph in the boxing rules to broaden the definition of the word foul.

BOXING AND ENTERTAINMENT

In order to become a world boxing champion, a boxer must possess the following attributes: Be fearless, mean, a perfect physical specimen, have a very hard head, be a super athlete and, most importantly, be highly intelligent, since the ability to concentrate is not innate, and it's a skill that must be developed (I write about mental discipline in Chapter 6). Boxing is not a sport for the timid. Most of the rules that I have looked at do not address the safety of the boxer. As I noted above, the objective of the sport is to disable an opponent by administering mayhem. Since it's impossible to knock a head off with a blow from a fist, no one worries. In boxing the words health, safety and wellbeing are used by politicians who have little to no experience in the art of fighting with the fist.

In the boxing rules there is only one paragraph which addresses the safety of the downed boxer. It states: "In the event of a knock down the referee shall count to ten." Period. Nothing else. However, since the rules state that the referee is the only person who can interpret them, he will often end the count early to tend to the downed warrior. At that moment, it is not an important issue because the ring doctor will tell you that the prone position (lying flat with the chest down and back up) is best for the downed fighter until he is examined.

In a full bout without a knockout, the mystery that surrounds the decision gives the appearance of collusion or that the officials are dishonest or blind. The fans' discomfort with the decision is a function of the fact that they were concentrating on their fighter, and will see only the blows that are being delivered. The fan is like most seconds: they see only what their fighter is doing. They do *not* see what is coming; they have no knowledge of what is coming or why their boy is all beat-up. On numerous occasions, I asked the corner if they were ready to stop the fight, and the response that I received was an angry questioning look: "What are you talking about *referee*? We are winning the fight!" When in fact, their fighter was getting beat-up, sometimes badly.

The rules specify the size of the ring and nothing else. I saw a fight where the ring collapsed, therefore we need to protect the people on top of the ring. Those rules should also include specifications for the structure of the ring, and require it be erected on a level surface, as two huge fighters bouncing around could make the ring travel if it's on a slope. We also need stipulations for the volume of the ring bell, and for the method of signaling the ten-second warning. The level of the noise produced by fans is over 100 decibels, which is very loud, and in the very large arenas the noise level can be extremely loud. Therefore, the bell and the warning equipment should be rated in decibels of loudness.

Prior to the advent of television, a very large portion of the boxing fans was a sadistic crowd. Television brought a very large portion of a new kind of boxing fan, one who had to watch the fights but was not sadistic. Since they pay the bill, fans have the right to cast stones and burn up energy. If they are allowed to do that they will return to the fights. Boxing then becomes a form of entertainment that inherits a wide array of criticism from a fan that is not aware of the complexities of the boxing match. It's an event where 99.9 percent of the audience is unable to see what occurs in the ring... a ring with a referee and two fighters who chase each other all night.

In acknowledging the appreciation for what the television industry has done for the sport of boxing, we have branded the media and the boxing analyst as evil. Instead of sucking-up to them we, "the boxing officials must first get permission, from the commission, before they talk to the media," or we are counseled on what to say or not say. In the entertainment business we belong to the people, and the media is the avenue of our lifeblood; therefore, a muzzle on the officials is not a good idea. The speed and flow of the fight denies the referee the luxury of time to contemplate his actions, therefore criticism will always occur. With experience, the criticism of the officials will diminish but will always be there because there has never been two fights that were the same. The media thrives on *screw-ups* so the consequence is not always a bad thing, especially since the consequence is usually temporary in nature. I saw a fight where one of the fighters died the evening after his fight because the referee did not speak Spanish. That official did not know that professional fighters do not give up or quit, and that referee is still around. Most of the time it's called experience because it's easier to retrain the official then to start with a new one. When we are calculating the score cards on a fight that goes the distance, we hoard the television time because it takes us an average of five minutes to announce the mysterious and magical decision, and we need to include the television sector in our planning, so that we know what they need or how we can help them; after all they are only paying the bills. Despite the fact that amateur boxing experience is a liability to professional boxing, the amateur officials were smart enough to realize the value of electronics. They have computerized their scoring system and now tabulation is instant and the arithmetic is flawless, therein the outcome of the fight can be announced in seconds. The amateur officials computerized in order to eliminate the liability that is part of the responsibility, and they also disrupt the boxer's ability to learn how to concentrate when they demand instant compliance to their screams and theatrical gyrations. The amateur officials need to read the chapter on mental discipline in this book.

In the last 50 years, I have seen only two occasions when the commission scrutinized the outcome of a contest. The reality is that the referee's actions are never challenged or overruled by the commission, and I'm not saying that that's a good environment to be in. It only means that in the last hundred years, boxing has not had one single CEO at the helm. The CEO is a person of vision who understands that *change* means progress. A person must poses two attributes in order to qualify as a real CEO. First, he must be able to raise his arm and point a finger at someone, and then make a request. Secondly, that person must then be able to implement an effective follow-up plan. The truth is that if there's no follow-up nothing gets done.

The television punch statistics report and the amateur boxing scoring system are changes that are stunningly worthless. The statistics are similar to the sport of fencing where a touch—with the point of the epee'—indicates instant bleeding. This is similar to the amateur scoring system where a touch, with the glove, is the only thing that counts. This scenario is a serious liability to professional boxing because it instills a habit, one that the conditioned reflex will use when one is in a battle that is out of control. A battle is out of control when the fighter runs out of gas or is getting a beating.

Lastly, I would also like to mention—in terms of safety—the disposable rubber or latex gloves that are being used by referees for protection against AIDS: they are a waste of money. Doctor and author Lorraine Day states that the virus which causes AIDS is 50 times smaller than the pores on the gloves, and if the virus becomes aerosol it will contaminate everybody, at the ring side, in every direction.

1

MY STORY

When I was in High School, me and five other mischievous hooligans by the name of Henry, Che, Joe, Mike and Chevi, would regularly go watch the boxing matches at the Phoenix Madison Square Garden, a popular arena in downtown Phoenix at the time. The fan-base for boxing was so large that the Fire Marshall would close the doors of the arena when it was stuffed with at least 2,500 fans. At that day-in-time the population of Phoenix was approximately 50,000.

My pals and I would pull our resources and buy one balcony ticket to attend the fights. One of us entered the arena with the ticket and would slowly meander to the far corner of the balcony, and then stand in front of a small window that was always locked. Meanwhile, the rest of the gang would go to the alley behind the building that was next to the arena, and climb up to the roof, which was about two feet below the small balcony window. Inside the arena, the balcony "group of one" in front of the window would slowly grow to six spectators.

After school, this same group of friends liked to go watch the professional boxers and wrestlers workout at the Top Level Gym on South Central Avenue, in Phoenix. The gym was run by Paavo Ketonen—a boxing and wrestling promoter and also a former wrestler—and Paul Clinite—a boxing promoter at Madison Square Garden. The "pests" were there so often that the owners kind of liked us because we appeared to be seriously interested in what these professionals were all about. We were certain that the wrestlers were faking the shows, but we could see that these professional athletes had to work very hard in order to sufficiently fool the fans, and stay in good shape.

We had another unofficial member in our group that would regularly show up everywhere we gathered. We didn't know his name, and for some reason none of us ever asked him what his name was. He was not very tall, and we were certain that he was a little bit older than us. We addressed him as *"Paletas"*—the Spanish word for lollypop— because his mannerisms, his clothing and manner of speaking hinted to us that he was a homosexual. We guessed that he liked us because we were never mean to him. Occasionally, one of us would yell at him and tell him: "Shut up Paletas!" But he was never told to leave or go away. We didn't know where he lived or where he came from, and no one ever asked, so when he disappeared or stopped following us, we didn't worry about him.

Back at the gym, Clinite started "plotting" against us, the gang. He told us he was in need of six mean, fearless gentleman, and wanted to know if anyone in the group knew where he could find these type of men.

"What for?" We finally asked.

Clinite stated that he needed six gladiators to go fight the inmates at the "pen," the Arizona State Prison Complex, in Florence, Arizona. And then, the questions began flowing:

"Where's Florence?"

"How far is it?"

"What's an inmate?"

"Is the 'pen' the prison?"

"How much does it pay?"

The bottom line was, there was no pay. "But I will take you and bring you back," Clinite offered. "I will buy all your equipment: trunks, shoes, mouth-piece, and you get a big steak after the show."

After three hundred questions and no satisfactory answers, we agreed that the clincher was the big steak, a real rarity for us. We also told him we wanted to get a little schooling or training before the fight, managed by Clinite's best boxer.

The big day arrived, which turned into a day we never forgot. Each one of us agreed that the tall fences at the prison complex were wired and kind of scary. We also concluded that the inmates would not kill any of us due to the possibility of being kept locked up in that terrible-looking place for life. Later, we also deduced that the inmates were also warned that if they killed "anyone of them," there would be hell to pay and no more boxing shows.

My friend Henry was the first one in the ring. The inmates were on three sides and my friends and I were all on the other side. To this day, Henry still insists that he fought a "gorilla," an inmate twice as large as a gorilla. The whole show was at the ringside with no other than our long-lost friend "Paletas." When he saw Henry jump into the ring he went "bananas," elbowing the man next to him and screaming.

"That's my lover on the outside! Henry, honey, kick him, hit him, bite him, kill him baby!" And on, and on, and on he continued the theatrics, jumping up and down just like a chimp. Meanwhile, Henry was getting angry at "Paletas," and was yelling back at him: "Shut up 'Paletas' or I'm coming down there to kick your butt!" Of course, Henry didn't say "butt;" he used a more appropriate adjective. At the same time, the "gorilla" in the ring was fighting with Henry like a war machine, all over Henry, but my friend was so mad at "Paletas" that the blows coming from the gorilla just bounced off of him. Years later, Henry still claimed that "Paletas" saved all of us because he would have slaughtered the "gorilla" that beat him up, and then the jail officers would have kept us all locked up in there.

When the Korean War broke out in June of 1950, the entire gang of hooligans joined the U.S. Army, except me. I told the rest of my friends that I would follow them after finishing high school. I had other plans: I wanted to be one of the first men to fly to the Moon. That plan changed when I learned that the first men on the journey to the Moon would be by aeronautical engineers, and that the first attempt would be fatal to them. One of the hooligans did not return from Korea, one was captured but he escaped, and another passed away around 2000 from the result of wounds he received in the Korean War.

AGENT ORANGE

In 1952, I was attending the University of Arizona in Tucson. To pay my way through college I had three jobs, one of them was fighting boxing matches for my old friend Paul Clinite, who promoted professional boxing in Tucson, Yuma and Mexico. The pay was 50 bucks for a four rounder. I was fighting because I needed the money, but the only bad part of those fights was that the headaches sometimes lasted from one fight to the next one. In Mexico a boxer cannot dive or pretend that he is fighting because he can't fool the fans. I stopped counting the number of fights I lost at seventeen. During that time I also learned that the pay for the referee was 75 bucks per night.

In 1953, I joined the Army to get the GI Bill. I was discharged in 1956 from the Army's 82nd Airborne Division. The Vietnam War had begun a year earlier in 1955. In 1962, I worried that the Army would call me back, so I joined the 161st Aerial Refueling Wing of the Arizona Air National Guard that year. The reserve military force immediately sent me to a loadmaster school in Wisconsin. The loadmaster plays an essential role because he controls the weight of everything that is loaded into the airplane to prevent it from flying out of balance. The center of gravity has to be over the wings. I served as a loadmaster on the Boeing C-97 Stratofreighter, and later as the boom operator on the Boeing KC-135 Stratotanker. This unit travelled all over the world. When the war broke out, our National Guard unit, the 161st Air Refueling Group, was informed that it would be activated by the U.S. Air Force, unless we could give them the support that they needed. In order to comply, the unit provided the Air Force with two of our nine birds that would fly every day, back and forth, to the war zone. The C-97 is a big fat cargo airplane with 90 feet of cargo space. We would haul anything needed in the war effort from Travis Air Force Base in the San Francisco Bay Area to Vietnam.

Most of those trips from Phoenix took about ten days. We flew that route for about five years. On one of my trips there we delivered the cargo to Da Nang—a coastal city in central Vietnam—and on the first leg of our return trip, on the way to Guam, I passed out. When I awoke I could hear three doctors that were very near talking. They were in accord: none had ever seen this condition before. One of them stated that it resembled a case of scarlet fever (also called scarlatina) he had seen, but this one was one hundred times worse. I opened my eyes and I giggled to myself. The three doctors that were standing next to me, on my right, all dressed in white, and they resembled the Three Stooges. The farthest of the three had a hooked nose, the middle one was half bald-headed, and the third doctor had a mop on top of his head. Someone to my left had their attention; they were looking straight ahead, when I talked to them.

"What are you guys doing to me?" I asked.

They were all startled. Like woolen puppets they all looked down at me. Their eyes were as big as owls', and their mouths were wide open. Then, their heads turned real fast, looking at each other; they were dumfounded and flabbergasted. The one at the end, the one with the hooked nose, asked me: "How do you feel?"

"I feel as if you are sticking me with a thousand needles," I said.

Again, the "puppets" rolled their heads, looking at each other, as if wondering what to do. The one at the end raised his arm and pointed at someone. "Pick him up, put him on that table, dry him and then cover him with a mountain of blankets," he ordered. The three doctors moved out of the way and eight long arms reached under me and lifted me up. I was naked in a tub full of ice. In less than one minute I was moved, dried, and covered with blankets. All the arms moved away and the "three stooges" returned to my side. Their demeanor had changed to hope. And they waited and waited without saying anything. In just a few moments the heat from the blankets started to make me feel better.

"Thanks a lot fellows, I'm starting to feel better," I said.

Instantly, they all jumped with fists high in the air, and cheered; two had tears in their eyes. And then one hundred questions followed:

"What's your name?"

"How did you get here?"

"Where did you come from?"

"How long were you there?"

"Were you shot at?"

"Were you scared?"

They never left my side, taking turns watching me. Later that evening my crew showed up.

"What's wrong with him doc?" They asked.

"We don't know, we have never seen this condition before," one of the doctors said.

"How long will he be here?" They asked.

"Two or three weeks. If he gets another attack like this one he won't make it; his heart will not survive another attack like this one," the doctor said.

The following day the crew showed up again; now they were worried. It would take two or three weeks to find another loadmaster, and the base was thinking about pushing our aircraft into the ocean because it was in the way. So they pleaded, "If he will die from another attack, it will make no difference where he dies, will it?" They asked. "Let us have him. We will do his job on the airplane, and take good care of him. If necessary we can drop him off in Hawaii." So away we went.

A few years later, the Veterans Administration stated that the cause of my condition was the "Agent Orange"—one of the herbicides and defoliants used by the U.S. military as part of its herbicidal warfare program during the Vietnam War. Several of the unit members passed away from cancer or from exposure to the Agent Orange. I eventually retired from the National Guard after flying for 30 years.

I'd like to add that while serving in the Arizona Air National Guard, I became a Double Distinguished Marksman. I earned the Distinguished Marksmanship medals with a pistol and with the rifle. The 45 caliber automatic is used for the pistol badge, and the 30 caliber M1 rifle is used for the rifle badge. This award is the most coveted award in competitive bullseye marksmanship. It was started in 1884 and each medal is numbered. My pistol award is number 213 and was earned in 1978. The rifle badge was earned in 1984 and is number 193. In 1984, I became the 14th member of the National Guard to become Double Distinguished. These medals are 10-karat gold and contain two and one-half ounces of gold each. I earned a third badge in high school with a smallbore .22 rifle.

BECOMING A PROFESSIONAL REFEREE

In 1959, Jay Edson was the Boxing Executive Director in Arizona, a member of the Executive Board of the World Boxing Council (WBC), which is based in Mexico City. He was also the manager of the Maryvale Mall, a shopping center that used to be in West Phoenix. The director's job was a volunteer position with no pay, so all Edson needed was a job that had an office where he could conduct Boxing Commission's business. One day in the middle of the week, I walked into his office and handed him a lengthy resume of my experience as a boxer, and asked for a license to referee. Edson took one look at my resume and he could tell that it was slightly inflated. He then told me that he was in a bind for that coming weekend: he had a fight scheduled in Tucson and he needed a referee. "If you go and work that fight I'll consider your application. If something goes wrong it won't be a big deal because no one knows you down there," he told me. In those days, the promoter was required to schedule a minimum of 28 rounds of boxing in every show. So I went to Tucson and worked the entire show. On Monday morning I walked into his office and I asked him, "How did I do?"

"They called me a little while ago," he said. "They didn't say how you did, but they want you to go work their next fight in Yuma, which is next week."

I traveled the 200 hundred miles southwest from Phoenix to Yuma, and worked the entire card. That is how my career as a professional boxing referee began. In those days, the referee was also the third judge, and the pay was still 75 bucks per night.

One of my most memorable fights occurred at the Riverside Ballroom on South Central Avenue, in Phoenix. Eventually the venue was razed to give way to the Interstate 17 Highway. I was working the main event as the referee. It appeared to me that the promoter of the fight had gone to skid row to find his gladiators, and forgot to school them on how to throw a fight. In the first round, one of the boxers dramatically threw himself to the canvas without being struck by a blow. He landed about three feet from a tall professional basketball player that was at the ringside with his elbows resting on the canvas. I recollect that his name was Lucas. I sent his opponent to a corner, and then knelt down next to the guy, who was flat on his backside. I poked him in the chest, he opened his eyes and looked at me with a question in his eyes. I asked him why he was lying on the canvas. The downed boxer then told me that he had been hit. I then told him that if the referee did not see the blow that it did not count, therefore he must get up and continue the fight. A few seconds later he landed on his backside in the same spot, again without being hit. Once again I poked him in the chest and told him to "get up," and warned him that the next time that he went down without getting hit I would ask the Commission to put him and his trainer in jail. By this time Lucas was rolling with laughter. Seconds later he was hit by a glancing blow, and again landed on his backside, exactly at the very same spot. By this time, he and the fans at the ringside were all rolling on the floor laughing. Before I could poke him in the chest he opened his eyes, pointed a finger at me and explained, "I was hit this time!" Prior to this fight I had not reviewed the rules of the game with this boxer, so I allowed him to stay down.

In another fight, an amateur boxer was making his first professional fight. His opponent turned out to be a war machine and promptly drove him into the floor, where I counted him out. Sometime after the show, the downed fighter cornered me, pointed a finger at me and told me that I was a dangerous referee that would allow someone to get killed while in the ring. I then explained to him that in amateur boxing, his mama and the referee protected him, and that in professional boxing his mama was not allowed in the ring, and that the referee would allow him to get up from a knockdown several times before he would stop the fight. That boxer never showed up for his second professional fight.

A controversial fight I refereed on October 9, 1990 at La Mancha

Athletic Club, in Phoenix, made me infamous forever as the worst professional boxing referee. In the Alex Garcia vs. Bernard Benton fight—televised live nationally on USA Cable—the fans claimed that I allowed Benton to get a good whipping, and that I should have stopped the fight before Garcia threw 32 unanswered punches. In my own defense, I want to consider that I knew some things about the match that others did not: Benton was a former World Boxing Council Cruiserweight champion, and part of The Ring magazine's ratings, who was attempting to make a comeback after losing the WBC championship in 1986, and another previous fight in 1987. I had these facts in my mind, so I was thinking that Benton needed to understand that this was his last chance to regain the title. He was a barber by trade and I thought he had to realize that a shot at the title was not within reach. I felt that the fight had to teach Benton that his career as a professional boxer was over, so I allowed the fight to continue until he fell, face down on the canvas. In title fights it's not unusual for the fighters to agree to wave the three-knock-down rule, so that there's no doubt on which boxer is victorious.

There are certain attributes that are imperially essential to becoming a world boxing champion, and most gladiators never get the opportunity to compete at that level. A boxer must be a perfect physical athlete, and must have a cranium that is able to withstand physical trauma. As a boxer myself, after each fight, I would develop a headache that would last for two weeks. A contender cannot become a champion if he gets headaches every time he fights. One must be physically coordinated and, most of all, be highly intelligent. If a fighter is not highly intelligent he will not be able to concentrate, because it's an attribute that is critically important in any competitive endeavor. In the essential needed skills of a short gladiator, such as in the case of Benton, a boxer has to understand that when his opponent is taller than him, his reach will enable him to beat him up from left field, therefore he must develop a plan to overcome that obstacle. Benton (5' 11½") was much shorter then Garcia (6' 2"). His plan was to get inside, so how do you do that without getting hit? It can't be done. Real quick a boxer finds out how hard his opponent can hit; if his opponent doesn't hit hard he will be allowed to land a few hits. Every time that he hits him, he knows that he is close enough so that his reach is within range. So a shorter boxer needs to sucker a taller boxer in until he becomes complacent and relaxes his guard, at that time he then returns a haymaker—a wild swing with all of a boxer's might to knock out the opponent.

In this battle Benton was in complete control up to the last ten seconds of the round. Champions learn how to roll with a punch; you see the punch coming and when it lands you roll away from it, just like a shock absorber, and it does not slow you down. Benton was waiting for the "war machine" in front of him to run out of gas, but Garcia did not run out of gas. In the last five seconds of the fight Garcia landed three solid punches that floored Benton. I knelt down and reached Benton, instructed him that the fight was over and that he should relax. Benton rolled over and the show started: everybody that wanted to be seen on the TV was instantly inside the ring. Benton got beat up in his own corner but sometimes things happen so fast that no one in his corner thought about jumping into the ring to help him. In the Far East, things like that occur all the time; a trainer or second will jump into the ring to help his fighter. The rules in boxing are specific and clear: "In the event of a knockdown the referee shall count to ten;" he does not have to call the ring doctor or call 911. The referee's job is over. The Commission, the ring doctor or the trainer can call for help if they desire. In that fight, no one did. A week after the fight, Sean O'Grady, a former boxer and the ring analyst, visited Benton at his barber shop and he found him in very good spirits and working away with his clients.

Six years later, I was the referee for the Terry Norris vs. Jorge Luis Vado match, a world title fight held at the Veterans Memorial Coliseum. The event was televised live nationally on USA Network on January 27, in 1996, the day before the Super Bowl XXX in Phoenix. Terry was an attraction because he had whipped Sugar Ray Leonard in 1991. This fight was important because it drew a very high rating on the Nielsen Ratings, which meant that the fight was viewed by a record number of viewers for a boxing match. An announcer told me that approximately 50 million fans worldwide watched the fight. Norris stopped the Nicaraguan boxer at 42 seconds of the second round to retain his World Boxing Council and International Boxing Federation junior middleweight titles.

I have refereed approximately 3,110 fights over the span of various decades. My online record as a referee, as detailed in the website Boxrec.com, lists only 77 of those bouts. The first fight registered is the match between Manny Elias vs. Ramiro Yaqui Nides held at the Star Theater in Phoenix on May 26, 1965. The last recorded one was a fight between Jesus Gonzales vs. Chance Leggett at the Fort McDowell Casino in Fountain Hills, Arizona on April 4, 2005. I worked fights that include outstanding World Champions Sugar Ray Leonard and Arizona native Michael Carbajal.

A New Method of Scoring Boxing

In 1965, The Ring magazine reported that the attendance at the fights in New York City and in California was down to 500 fans, and in Phoenix we were down to 300. That condition worried me. I thought real soon we would be in a similar scenario as in amateur boxing, where the fans are the relatives of the fighters, and it's a place where the officials don't realize that the referee interferes with the fighters' ability to learn how to concentrate. They thrive on the limelight; everything that they do is intended so that the fans know who the officials are. For that and other reasons, the individual's amateur boxing experience is a serious liability to his professional boxing career. Amateur boxing does not understand that when a gladiator suffers from a concussion or has a mental-relapse, his mind goes blank. When this occurs, your subconscious survival instincts take over and you perform exactly in accordance to the training that you received while training in the gym.

Thereafter, I laid out a plan to figure out the reason why boxing fans had disowned them. I compared boxing with all the other professional sports. My study revealed several glaring differences between boxing and the other sports:

1. The other sports do not have ties or draws; a team or a competitor is always victorious.

2. Their pay is a function of who is victorious; in boxing the pay is established before the fight takes place.

3. In boxing the fighter is paid to show up; he signs a contract to fight but sometimes he does not fight, and at the end of the show he still gets paid.

4. In all other sports the score is open and public throughout the entire contest, and the outcome of the contest is instantly known; in boxing there is no transparency and the scoring is classified as "top secret," and conducted by judges that possess a "super magical" ability to score a battle, one that supposedly the fan does not possess.

5. The second wind in athletics is always a factor in the outcome of the contest, except in boxing; in boxing when you run out of gas, there is *no* second wind so you get a good whipping.

I then selected what I thought was the most important difference between all other sports and boxing, and presented a plan of minor changes to the members of the Arizona Boxing Commission. At that time the Commissioners were: Shannon, Warren, Quihuis, and Pena. The plan consisted of open scoring. In 1966, during a few months' period, the plan was tried. The plan was so successful that the fans roared and cheered, and they approved it by 85 percent. The change was so positive that in December of 1967, the Commission adopted the Yanez Three-Point-Must system as the official method of scoring boxing in Arizona. In the first three fights the fan base climbed from 400 to 1,700. All the media was watching and they were all very critical. However, the day before the fourth fight a new Commission announced that open scoring was being suspended. The card had a rated heavyweight fighter, Tony Doyle, on the main event. The number of fans dropped to 500, and there it stayed.

Even though the new Commission had not even seen it in action, the new scoring system was dropped, arguing that we were members of the WBC, and that our new scoring system violated their rules. I questioned their actions and Dr. Shannon (the Chair), responded that the arithmetic of the new system was too complicated, and would have to be improved before we tried it again. Since the highest number in the system is a three, I concluded that we would never return to the open scoring with the new Commission. It appears that resistance to change is one of the tragedies that interferes with progress. Therefore, the main reason that boxing has faded away is that it has never experienced *change*.

The Arizona Boxing Commission has three members and one member changes every year, therefore we have a completely new Commission every three years. From 1968 to 2005, I showed the history of the three-point must to most of the new commissioners in hope that they would again consider open scoring, but that did not occur. In about 1980 a new executive director, John Montano, came on board. He feared change, unless the change was his own idea, so open scoring was out of the question. Since the director's position had no pay attached to it, he could do pretty much what he wanted. Montano was so ruthless that on the Internet he is known as "King John."

A perennial complaint that I had with the director was that the referee's pay was too low. In 1952, the pay for the referee was $75 per show, and by the year 2005 the pay had climbed backward to $70 per show. He would always tell me that boxing was a hobby for the officials, and therefore they would never get a raise.

Around 2004, Mary Rose Wilcox, who at the time was a member of the Maricopa County Board of Supervisors, was appointed to the Boxing Commission. At the ringside I gave her the first lesson on how to score a fight. I knew her from when she first ran for a political office. Some friends and I had helped her in her first political endeavor, and she was also a regular boxing fan. Since I knew her so well, I deduced that open scoring would become a reality... But I was wrong! She "fell in love" with the director because she enjoyed the exposure that she would get at all the fights. Since the director did not like any of the changes that I recommended, I was dead in the water, because she would always support him. Despite this, I harbor no animosity toward these folks.

Any person who believes that professional boxing is dangerous needs to watch an Ultimate Fighting Championship contest (UFC). I believe that people will agree that professional boxing is nothing when compared to a UFC contest.

I worked for the City of Phoenix for 30 years. During that period I diligently followed a philosophical plan for improving the workplace: The first year on the job was to learn about the duties of that department. The second year was to do the work that was required. On the third year was to give back to the department by making it a better place than when I started, if possible, and then move on to a different department, even if it meant a reduction in pay. In all those moves I took a reduction in pay only once. I tried to do the same thing for professional boxing, and I almost succeeded. I will not return to the sport of boxing unless I can somehow help revive it.

These are the minor administrative changes that I propose, which don't change or alter the system of fisticuffs:

1. Open scoring; announce the score and show it on the scoreboard where everybody can see it.

2. Computerize the scoring system; the amateurs do it and they use five judges.

3. The pay for boxers can never be equal; the fighter who is victorious has to receive more pay. The pay is the motivating drive that will revive the second wind in the warriors. In matches that customarily require a guaranteed purse, the guarantee shall be honored *only* if the boxer is victorious; if he loses the fight the purse shall go to his opponent.

The above pay structure will eliminate fixed fights. Those fights are fights that generate rematches, and are conceived by businessmen in the entertainment business. We all have seen them. It is not uncommon for two world champions to battle for twelve rounds, and emerge with an unmarked face. Why should they get hurt when the purse is guaranteed? Does it make sense? Yes, because they are businessmen who don't have to engage in fisticuffs.

The complete history of the open scoring system is described in chapter eight.

ARIZONA BOXING COMMISSION

The Arizona Revised Statutes state that the Boxing Commission shall regulate the sport of boxing; have three commissioners in office for a term of three years; the Chair is always the one in his third year in office. These statutes mean that the Commission shall observe all the events, and make sure that everybody complies with the rules. However, since the commissioners are all members of the private sector, the oversight is not obvious, and because John Montano, who previously headed the commission for approximately 30 years, micromanaged and ruled with an iron-fist. On the Internet he was known as "King John."

The last two boxing directors, Mr. Dennis O'Connell and Mr. Matt Valenzuela, came from amateur boxing, therefore what is left of professional boxing in Arizona is now frothed with the amateur syndrome of bad habits and theatrics. The amateur boxer has to worry about his opponent and a referee that is constantly demanding instant compliance to his commands, that likes to hold hands with both gladiators in the middle of the ring at the end of all his battles, and that stops the fight at the sight of blood or when one of the boxers appears to be hurt. Toward the end of this chapter I elaborate on amateur boxing referees.

The Boxing Commission is obligated to teach new boxers who aspire to enter the professional boxing arena that this sport is not for the weak or timid. The director can help this endeavor by assigning experienced referees to work the newbies. When to stop or not to stop a fight is the key element to training new referees. If a referee stops the fight too soon, the fighter might not learn that this profession can be very unforgiving, and if he allows the fight to continue too long, the boxer might get hurt. The experienced referee will make the best decision... most of the time.

The Arizona rules infer and imply that the referee is in charge, and the Arizona Boxing Commission (ABC) states: "The Referee shall be the only person that can interpret the rules." Therefore, no one else should evaluate the performance of the referee, especially if they do not have refereeing experience. That job belongs to the director.

On October 29, 2005, at the Desert Diamond Casino in Tucson, Arizona, John Montano, ABC's former director, brought three out-of-state referees to work sanctioned title boxing fights. Montano's action constituted gross mismanagement, and it indicated that he did not have competent officials to represent the State of Arizona. It's the job of the director to provide adequate training for his officials.

Montano always stated that boxing is a hobby for the state's officials and, therefore, their pay has always been very low. The sanctioning authority for title fights establishes the amount of pay for the fight's officials, a pay scale that is considerably more than for club fights runs, which range from an average of 1,000 to 5,000 dollars per fight. So when the director brings in out-of-state officials to work those fights, it gives the appearance of collusion or that the state officials are not experienced or competent enough to work big fights.

In the private sector personnel mismanagement is a way-of-life, completely, without oversight. However, when the executive director became an Arizona government employee, he inherited the Administrative Code, which he must follow. That code states that mismanagement, abuse of authority or reprisals are a capital offense. Adequate personnel management requires a job description for all the boxing officials. Without a job description, conditions of employment for the officials do not exist, therefore rules or conditions of employment are imaginary, since those rules are not documented.

Nothing moves without the approval of the commission's director. He approves and disapproves every single contestant, so when there's a mismatch it's the Commission's fault, not the promoter's. Consequently, the referee then has to deal with a mismatch, and clean it up as best as he can. The Arizona rules state that a matchmaker can be censured when he makes fights that are a mismatch, so the Commission should not be approving and disapproving contestants; that's the job of the matchmaker. Federal laws prohibit discrimination due to a boxer's age. However the Arizona Boxing Commission routinely forces boxing license applicants who are too old to beg for a license at their meetings.

The Arizona Statutes never mention the word *safety*. The only sentence in those statutes that addresses the safety of the fighter states: "In the event of a knockdown the referee shall count to ten," which means that the ring doctor cannot jump into the ring to see if the boxer is dead. He has to wait until the referee has ended the count or is called into the ring by the referee.

In the Introduction I mentioned another important aspect of boxing: the need for specifications for the bell and for the device being used for signaling the ten-second warning. I said that the bell—or what is used—to sound the ten-second warning signal should show that the sound level exceeds 100 decibels. This is essential because Montano charged me with being inapt for not stopping a fight after the bell sounded, and thereafter suspended my license as a referee. The fight took place on April 29, 2005 between boxers Victor Maciel and George Garcia at the Glendale Arena, in Glendale, Arizona. During my suspension's appeal, in a private hearing, the videotapes of the fight in question clearly showed that the director had made a wrong decision. The sound level was so loud that I could not hear the bell, and I may have not heard the ten-second warning signal either. The video was shot from above the ring at an angle where the entire ring could be seen. From this vantage point, the activities of everybody at the ringside could also be seen. The director had not noticed that the video clearly showed that the timekeeper, Mr. Bill Buck, sounded the ten-second warning, and then ten seconds later he sounded the bell that ended the round. At that moment the referee was not needed because the gladiators heard the bell, they both stopped fighting, and then went to their respective corners. This all occurred because the director—who sits at the ringside—can see only the top of the head of his employees that are on the other side of the ring; he couldn't see what they were doing, and because he did not understand the reasons for having a ten-second warning signal. The warning signal is a device that is different from the bell; it can be a horn, a whistle, or a hand that slaps the canvas when the referee can see the timekeeper.

The referee could do a better job of regulating the flow of the show if he could use the one minute rest period between rounds. That time is not available because he has to run around collecting scorecards. At most of the shows, the third man in the ring has to admonish behavior, usually a fighter's or his trainer's. Adequate personnel management suggests that admonishment is more effective if it is conducted in private. Therefore, the best time to talk to the corner folks would be during the one minute rest period between rounds because the fans can't hear conversations in the ring, and are not looking at the ring activities during that time. This is another good reason why scoring should be conducted electronically. During that time the referee will have more time to better regulate the action in the ring.

The boxer's owner and trainer are the only persons who have an innate interest in the health and safety of the fighter. They are the only ones aware of existing health conditions or other factors that could affect the performance of their fighter, or conditions that could worsen during a fight. Therefore, the rules should give the fighter's corner the authority to stop the contest by throwing the towel into the ring. Existing rules do not address the safety of the warriors, and it should not be the sole responsibility of the referee; the ring doctor and the boxer's owner should bear that as an obligated responsibility.

Prior to 2006, boxing fans in Arizona were viewing approximately

25 fights per year. One of the boxing promoters was SRL Promotions, which was promoting fights at the Desert Diamond Casino in Tucson. One of the first things that occurred which led to the demise of boxing in Arizona began when it appeared that the director of the Boxing Commission excluded SRL Promotions from the state.

In 2007, the Arizona State Legislature noticed that the Ultimate Fighting Championship (UFC) was developing a very large fan base, which meant revenues for the State, consequently leading to the demise of boxing. A bill appeared in the legislature for the approval of cage fighting, and the Commission jumped on it. They stated that the new law would jeopardize the safety of the fighters, and could result in serious injuries or death. In September 2008, the Legislature approved the Mixed Martial Arts (MMA), so the Commission was forced to like it, especially since boxing is still dormant. MMA's fighters are all making money, and the sport is just as safe as boxing. It might even be safer because the fighters are better conditioned than boxers.

Currently, the director is not an employee of the Boxing Commission but a government employee of the State who works for the Arizona Department of Racing—which "regulates and supervises all boxing, kickboxing, tough man, and mixed martial arts events in Arizona to ensure compliance with laws and regulation and, thereby, protect all participants." Therefore, the new director has inherited the State's Administrative Code. The Code—Title 38-532—clearly states that the integrity of all employees shall be beyond reproach, and that mismanagement and abuse of authority are capital offenses; a large fine and dismissal is the consequence.

For some strange reason, the sport of boxing has been damned with people who live in a vacuum. Boxing has stagnated, and state officials aren't aware of it; they are satisfied with a big funeral therein "let us just find something else to do; maybe we can go watch golf?" If two minor administrative changes are made, boxing can be turned into a very lucrative sport. These two changes and others I propose are outlined in the chapter about open scoring.

Another change needed is the fiduciaries. The boxer that is

victorious always gets the big trophy, all or most of the money. In most main events, the best gladiator usually wants a guaranteed purse, and that's okay. However, he must be victorious or the purse goes to the person that whips him.

AMATEUR BOXING REFEREES

In Arizona, the Amateur Boxing Association is in full control of professional boxing. To my knowledge, none have professional boxing experience. The current director is Mr. Matthew Valenzuela. Mr. Dennis O'Connell and Mr. Richard Soto are referees, both properly anointed as professional referees by the ABC. The political climate is the reason that they are in charge. The director seats at the pleasure of the State Governor, and when Montano retired, O'Connell was then appointed as the boxing director.

At this juncture, let's be clear about the Amateur Boxing Association. They are all honest, dedicated, hard workers, and committed to the sport of boxing. Historically, professional boxing has ostracized the amateur boxing officials due to their odd idiosyncrasies that identifies them as amateur officials while in the ring, such as the following habit: holding the hand of both warriors at the end of a contest in the middle of the ring, while waiting for the decision of the outcome of the battle. This action might prevent the fighter from running or defending himself if he is attacked or assaulted, as the ring can instantly become highly explosive.

In professional boxing, both contenders wait in their respective corners for the decision to be announced. When that occurs, the boxer who is victorious walks to the referee—who is in the middle of the ring—and the looser of that fight can sneak out of the ring if he is embarrassed, or he can go and congratulate the winner.

Amateur referees are, forever, in the middle of the ring with arms outstretched, as if waiting for a heard of wild bulls to pass, and while awaiting the sound of the bell that signals the start of the match. The referee then jumps out of the way, allowing the fight to begin. He should stand out of the way and just wait for the warriors to engage themselves when they hear the bell sound. It appears that these referees are constantly screaming meaningless words such as: "Watch your head! Stop! Or, box!" They are not aware that when in the middle of a battle, boxers are concentrating so hard that they cannot see or hear those instructions. And the meddling clown is a distraction to the fight. It appears that most of these actions by amateur referees are due to their need to be seen or noticed by the fans. This behavior, or posing for the media photographers, is one that the media does not like. They are not aware that when they stop moving during the battle, they are obstructing the view of many spectators, therefore an effective and professional referee must train his legs never to stop moving. Criticizing the new referees has to be done with temperament, since it is very difficult to create a good training program for them because there has never been two fights that were the same. Therefore, the subject is highly subjective.

It appears that the boxing commissions and the ABC are not aware that professional boxing is dead. They are satisfied with entertaining the fans by combining the amateurs with the professionals, and adding very loud noise and colored rotating lights, all night. My hearing aids were in the *off* position at a fight I attended on May 20, 2016, in Phoenix. There were 60 rounds of boxing, and an eight round "main event," a North American Boxing Federation (NABF) Junior Championship Title at stake: Francisco De Vaca, from Phoenix (record of 14-0) vs. Gustavo Molina, from Mexico, (record 22-11), who disputed a Super Bantamweight title fight. I'll give you one guess on who won this fight. You be the judge. Is this professional boxing or is it not?

On July 16, 2016, I paid $34.00 (general admission) for Professional Boxing at the Celebrity Theatre, sponsored by a local boxing promotion company. R-4-3-404-B of the State Boxing rules states: "Matchmakers will be held responsible for the making of mismatches. For the protection of the boxers and the public, the persistent making of mismatches is ground for the suspension or revocation of a matchmaker's license." We saw eight fights that night. Seven four round fights and one eight round main event. During the entire show I saw about fourteen warriors that had no professional boxing skills; five KO's, and a main event that was equally lopsided. If I were a member of the Arizona Boxing Commission, I would have suspended the promoter and revoked the matchmaker's license.

If you are still not convinced I'll give you some history. When I was in high school, the Phoenix Fire Marshall would close the door at the now defunct Phoenix Madison Square Garden when it was stuffed with approximately 2,500 fans, at a time, when the population of Phoenix was approximately 50,000. In 1966, the number of boxing fans had dropped to 300. Today, the population of the Phoenix area is 3.5 million and it appears to me that the paying fan base is about approximately 1,500. Today, all professional sports are drawing a minimum of 20,000 fans, sometimes three or four days in a row. My experience with open scoring in boxing indicates that when this method is adopted, the fan base will increase until it equals that of the other sporting events.

THE RULES

In Arizona no one knows the rules of boxing because they have never read them. The Commission should provide a copy of the rules to every licensee. The complete rules are available in the Arizona Administrative Code, and are published on the internet. In the following section I include some of these rules; the added recommended changes are italicized and in brackets:

STATE BOXING AND MIXED MARTIAL ARTS COMMISSION

TITLE 4. PROFESSIONS AND OCCUPATIONS CHAPTER 3. STATE BOXING AND MIXED MARTIAL ARTS COMMISSION

(Authority: A.R.S. § 5-221 et seq.)

HISTORICAL NOTE

Adopted effective January 21, 1981 (Supp. 81-1).

R4-3-305. REFEREE

A. The referee shall have direction and control over contestants and their seconds during a contest subject to the governing laws and rules.

He shall have final authority to decide if an injury is produced by a fair or foul blow and if an act is intentional or accidental. He shall have final authority to stop a contest when in his opinion a contestant is unfit to continue or otherwise cannot compete. *[The Referee is the only person that can interpret the Rules and Regulations.]*

B. In the case of a cut or other injury which the referee believes may be incapacitating, the referee may consult with the ringside physician before making a decision and may interrupt a round and have the clock stopped for this purpose.

C. Where a contestant is incapacitated because of a foul, the referee has the discretion to interrupt a round and have the clock stopped to enable the contestant to recover.

HISTORICAL NOTE

Adopted effective January 21, 1981 (Supp. 81-1).

ARTICLE 3. CONDUCT OF CONTESTS

R4-3-301. FAIR BLOWS AND FOULS

A. The only fair blow is one delivered with the padded knuckle part of the glove on the front or sides of the head and body above the belt.

B. All blows that are not fair as described in subsection (A) above are fouls. The following practices are also classified as fouls:

1. Hitting an opponent who is down or in the process of getting up after being down.

2. Holding an opponent with one hand and hitting with the other.

3. Holding or maintaining a clinch after directed by the referee to break.

4. Pushing or wrestling.

5. Butting with the head or shoulder.

6. Hitting on the break.

7. Hitting after the bell has sounded ending the round.

8. Any unsportsmanlike trick or action likely to cause injury to an opponent in the opinion of the referee.

9. Refusal to obey the commands of the referee.

10. Falling down intentionally.

[11. Dancing and running excessively.]

[12. Any action or movement that would not lead to mayhem, such as showboating.]

HISTORICAL NOTE

Adopted effective January 21, 1981 (Supp. 81-1).

R4-3-302. INTENTIONAL FOUL

A. The referee shall have discretion as to the penalty for fouling. He may direct the deduction of points and, in the case of persistent or major fouling, or where the foul incapacitates the victim of the foul from continuing, disqualify the wrongdoer. Normally, in the case of minor fouling, the referee should issue a warning before imposing a penalty. Penalties shall be imposed during or immediately after the round in which the foul occurs. The referee shall personally advise the corners and each judge of the points deducted immediately upon imposition of the penalty.

B. If a contestant is injured (e.g., cut) by an intentional foul but can continue, the referee shall notify the judges and the Commission representative at ringside that if the foul-inflicted injury is subsequently aggravated to the point that the injured contestant cannot continue, a technical win will be rendered in favor of the injured contestant if he is ahead on points, or the points are even, and a technical draw will be rendered if he is behind on points.

HISTORICAL NOTE

Adopted effective January 21, 1981 (Supp. 81-1).

R4-3-303. ACCIDENTAL FOUL

A. If a contestant is accidently fouled (e.g., butted) so that he cannot continue, the referee shall stop the contest and a technical decision shall be rendered in favor of the contestant ahead on points. If the points are even, or if the butt occurs in the first three rounds, a technical draw shall be declared.

B. If a contestant is injured (e.g., cut) by an accidental foul but can continue, the referee shall notify the judges and the Commission representative at ringside that if the foul-inflicted injury is subsequently aggravated to the point that the injured contestant cannot continue, the contest will be stopped and a technical win will be rendered in favor of the contestant ahead on points. If the points are even, or if the stoppage occurs in the first three rounds, a technical draw shall be declared.

HISTORICAL NOTE

Adopted effective January 21, 1981 (Supp. 81-1).

R4-3-304. SUBSTANCES

A. No drugs or stimulants may be given to a contestant within 24 hours preceding or during a contest.

B. Only plain water may be administered to a contestant during a contest.

C. Coagulants such as adrenalin 1/1000, and others expressly approved by the ringside physician, may be used between rounds to stop bleeding of cuts. "Iron type" coagulants, such as Monsel's solution are absolutely prohibited.

D. Small amounts of Vaseline may be used around the eyes.

E. Upon specific request of the Commission, a contestant shall provide a urine sample before and/or after a contest.

HISTORICAL NOTE

Adopted effective January 21, 1981 (Supp. 81-1).

R4-3-306. KNOCKDOWNS

A. When contestant is considered knocked down. A contestant is considered down when any part of his body but his feet is on the floor or he is on the ropes and unable to stand on his own, or he is knocked out of the ring.

B. Counting. When the contestant is knocked down the referee shall order the opponent to the farthest neutral corner of the ring, pointing to the corner. The count shall begin by the timekeeper immediately upon the knockdown. The timekeeper, by audible counting and hand signaling, shall give the referee the correct one-second interval for his count. The referee shall pick up and audibly announce the passing of the seconds, accompanying the count with appropriate hand motions. The referee's count is the official count.

C. Mandatory eight. A contestant who is knocked down shall not be allowed to resume boxing until the referee has finished counting eight. A contestant may take the count either on the floor or standing.

D. Neutral corner. Should the contestant causing a knockdown fail to stay in the farthest neutral corner during the count, the referee shall cease counting until the contestant has returned to that corner. The referee shall than go on with the count from the point at which it was interrupted.

E. Signaling. The referee shall wave both arms to indicate that a contestant has been counted out or cannot otherwise continue, and shall raise the hand of the opponent as the winner.

F. No saving by bell. Except in the last round, there is no saving by the bell. If a contestant is knocked down during the last ten seconds of a round, the count shall continue after the end of the round as if the round was not ended. The one minute rest period will begin from the time he rises after the knockdown. If a contestant is knocked down during a round, and counted out after the end of a round, the knockout shall be considered as having taken place during the round which was last finished.

G. Wipe gloves. Before a contestant resumes boxing after having been knocked, or having slipped, to the floor, the referee shall wipe any accumulated resin from the contestant's gloves before allowing the bout to resume.

H. Three knockdowns. Except in championship contests, upon

consent of both contestants and the Commission, when a contestant is knocked down for the third time in a round, the referee shall stop the contest and raise the hand of the opponent as the winner.

I. Knocked out of ring. A contestant who is knocked or fallen out of the ring, may be helped back onto the ring apron by anyone except his manager or seconds. He has a total of 20 seconds to get into the ring and rise.

J. Double knockout. A simultaneous double knockout shall be declared a technical draw.

HISTORICAL NOTE

Adopted effective January 21, 1981 (Supp. 81-1).

R4-3-307. CONDUCT OF SECONDS

A. A contestant may have up to three seconds and shall designate to the referee which of them is the chief second. The chief second is responsible for the conduct of the assistant seconds.

B. A second may not enter the ring or stand on the apron during the progress of a round. He may not administer aid to a contestant during a round. During an officially interrupted round, a second may stand on the apron only with the express permission of the referee.

C. Seconds must remain seated outside the ring between the progress of a round and must comport themselves in such a way as not to interfere with the progress of a round. The referee has the discretion to disqualify a second whose conduct is interfering with the contest.

HISTORICAL NOTE

Adopted effective January 21, 1981 (Supp. 81-1).

R4-3-308. METHOD OF JUDGING

A. Three judges shall score all contests. Under special circumstances two judges and the referee may score. The method of judging shall be the 10-point must system. In this system the better contestant receives 10 points and his opponent proportionately less, but not less than 7 points. If the round is even, each contestant receives 10 pounds. A fraction of points may not be given. Points for each round shall be awarded immediately after the termination of the round and not subsequently changed. Judges shall sign their scorecards.

B. The referee shall pick up the scorecards of the judges and then deliver the cards to the Commission representative assigned to check them for the mathematical accuracy. When the Commission representative has completed his checking he shall advise the announcer of the decision, and the announcer shall then inform the audience of the decision over the speaker system. The Commission representative shall stand at the ring apron when checking the scorecards.

[C. Electronics shall be used for scoring each round and the official cumulative score shall be announced over the speaker system at the end of each round.]

HISTORICAL NOTE

Adopted effective January 21, 1981 (Supp. 81-1).

R4-3-309. FAILURE TO RESUME BOXING AFTER REST PERIOD

The failure to resume boxing after a rest period shall be considered as if a knockout occurred in the next round.

HISTORICAL NOTE

Adopted effective January 21, 1981 (Supp. 81-1).

R4-3-310. MOUTHPIECE

A. Mouthpieces knocked out or spit out during the course of a round shall not be replaced until it can be done without interfering with the advantage the aggressor may have. As soon as it can be properly replaced, the referee shall direct a second to wash the mouthpiece and the referee shall then replace it with all deliberate speed.

B. A contestant who intentionally spits out his mouthpiece in an apparent attempt to cause the progress of a round to be interrupted is subject to penalty to be determined by a referee.

Historical Note

Adopted effective January 21, 1981 (Supp. 81-1).

Amended subsection A. Effective December 31, 1984 (Supp. 84-6).

Historical Note

Adopted effective January 21, 1981 (Supp. 81-1).

ARTICLE 4. ADMINISTRATION

R4-3-401. Age and physical condition of boxer applying for license

A. All contestants must have attained their eighteenth birthday before being licensed. No boxer over 32 years of age shall be granted a license except by special action of the Commission considering an applicant's demonstrated competence, status as a boxer and physical condition.

B. Any boxer applying for a license or renewal thereof must be examined by a Commission physician and satisfy the Commission that he has the ability to compete.

R4-3-402. Boxers injured

A. At the conclusion of a contest, the ringside physician shall enter the ring and examine and tend to a contestant who has been knocked out or is otherwise injured. The seconds of the injured contestant must not interfere with the physician.

B. Contestants who have been knocked down and out shall be kept in a prone position until they have recovered.

C. A contestant who has been knocked out shall not be permitted to compete until 30 days has elapsed or until such later time as a Commission physician and the Commission shall determine. The term "knockout" as used herein includes technical knockout.

D. A boxer who has been knocked out three consecutive times within the twelve month period preceding a scheduled contest will not be permitted to compete. The term "knockout" as used herein includes technical knockout.

HISTORICAL NOTE

Adopted effective January 21, 1981 (Supp. 81-1).

R4-3-407. SELECTION AND PAYMENT OF OFFICIALS *[AND FIGHTERS]*

A. The referee, judges, timekeepers, ringside physicians, and inspectors shall be selected by the Commission prior to the scheduled card and paid by a Commission representative, no later than immediately after the last scheduled contest in accordance with the Commission's fee schedule. The fee schedule shall be made known to the promoter before the scheduled card at such time as requested by the promoter.

B. A promoter or contestant may protest the assignment of officials only upon specific grounds submitted to the Commission in writing prior to the start of the scheduled card.

C. Referees shall be given a physician examination as determined by the ringside physician before officiating at a contest.

[D. The amount of pay for the fighters shall be approved by the Boxing Commission in all fights; the person that is victorious shall receive 50 percent more than the loser. In a fight that has a guaranteed purse amount, that purse shall be honored if he is victorious. If he loses a battle his opponent shall receive the purse.]

HISTORICAL NOTE

Adopted effective January 21, 1981 (Supp. 81-1).

R4-3-408. COMMISSION SEATING AT CONTESTS

The promoter is to provide a table and contiguous front row seating for the three members of the Commission and the executive secretary in the middle of one side of the ring where no judge is seated. The promoter is also required to provide front row seating for three judges, two timekeepers (one counting for the knockdowns), and two ringside physicians. The promoter is further required to provide ten ringside seats selected by him in the area where the Commission is seated, and within eye view and earshot of the Commission, for deputies, inspectors, judges, referees, and other officials assigned to work the scheduled card.

There are a couple of rules that need attention: "R4-3-302 Intentional foul A", and "R4-3-401 Age and physical condition of boxer applying for license A and B."

Rule R4-3-302 states that a blow below the belt is a foul. This rule needs to be reworded because no one wears a belt as part of their dress, therefore the belt-line is an imaginary location. Additionally, the boxing glove is approximately six-inches wide, so if the blow lands with the top portion of the glove, the bottom portion will be in the foul zone. Therefore, if the referee was watching the glove at the moment that it landed, he would have to stop the contest to pull out his measuring tape in order to determine if that blow was a foul or was not a foul. That sounds silly, doesn't it? Most of the time, the trunks are so high that they cover the belly button. The groin protector has a wide belt that holds the cup in place, and that belt is under the trunk's belt. A good upper-cut on the belt-line will pull up on the groin protector and render the gladiator an ambulance case. This instance is highly prevalent because fighters' cups are not custom-made. When a fighter lands a blow on the cup, the referee usually hears the pop because the cup is made of plastic. A blow to the groin can't be faked because it will immediately send the boxer to the hospital. Occasionally, a fighter will try to claim a low-blow, and when that occurs the referee has to use his own judgement, keeping in mind that in the heat of the moment a gladiator will not lie; most will tough it out because they are real warriors. In a case where the referee is not sure, he should step between the contenders, stare at the hurt boxer, with a questioning look, not saying anything and giving the fighter a chance to recover, especially if he is walking with a limp. On such occasions, the referee is not disrupting the flow of the contest, which is the most important part of his job. The modified rule should read as follows: *"A blow below the belt-line that renders the fighter incapacitated shall be considered a foul."*

Regarding Rule R4-3-401, the Commission routinely, and almost at every meeting, forces applicants for a license to fight to stand on the podium and defend their application. There are several reasons why this rule should be eliminated. First: adequate personnel management suggests that to discipline or embarrass persons in public constitutes mismanagement; secondly: discrimination based on age is forbidden by the Fifth and Fourteenth Amendments of the United States Constitution; and, thirdly: there are many reasons why we should allow the ring to determine one's proficiency. There are numerous world boxing champions that exceed those age limits. A friend of mine, Mr. Mac, was hiking into the Grand Canyon at the age of 90, and the end of the list can go on-and-on. Many of the boxing rules are written by illusions that the sport of boxing is a very dangerous sport, when as a matter of fact it is not one of the most dangerous. The UFC makes boxing look like a pussycat sport. There are only four MMA deaths registered in sanctioned fights, but the death rate is very low in this sport because they are all in super physical condition. In MMA fights anything goes, three things are forbidden: biting, eye-gouging, and hitting below the belt line. Most of the action occurs while the gladiators are on the canvas.

For the sake of fairness, I also cite research from the University of Alberta in Canada shows that MMA fighters end up with minor injuries than boxers. The study, "Combative Sports Injuries: An Edmonton Retrospective (2015), points out that "the overall injury incidence in MMA competitors appears slightly higher than for boxers, but MMA fighters experience more minor contusion/bruising injuries. Boxers are more likely to experience serious injury such as concussion/head trauma involving loss of consciousness or eye injury such as retinal detachment." The study used data from 2000 to 2013, and included 1,181 MMA competitors and 550 boxers.

The rules should also define the duties of the boxing judge: The duties of the boxing judge are to record the action or what occurs in the ring one round at a time as if it's the only round in the fight.

DEFINITIONS:

1. A punch that does not land or hit something is worth nothing.

2. A punch is a blow that lands anywhere on the opponent.

3. A hard punch is a blow that visibly staggers or shakes the opponent.

4. The objective of a boxing match is to administer mayhem within the parameter of the fight rules.

5. Dancing or theatrics is a foul.

I will further elaborate on the role of the boxing judge in the chapter titled: *The Boxing Judge*.

3

THE PROFESSIONAL BOXING REFEREE

The professional boxing referee is a unique fellow unlike any other arbitrator, arbiter, umpire or judge. He is the judge, jury and executioner in every boxing match. Therefore, the referee must frequently review the rule book and the chapter on concentration, since a fight is never stopped to review the rules.

The referee's decisions are never questioned even if he is wrong. Mistakes are based on the extent of experience the official has; the more experience he has the fewer mistakes he will incur. There has never been two fights that were alike; they are all different. The referee could get sick in the middle of a battle and not be aware of it; he could catch a cold and not know it. That could trigger the start of a bad day.

The referee controls the flow and temperament of the contest, especially during a fight that is being televised. He has to make decisions on the spur of the moment, without the luxury of time to contemplate his actions. He will make a decision and evaluate the quality of that decision after the fact. Due to the haste of events he will make mistakes, but the frequency of mistakes will diminish as the degree of experience he acquires increases. When in doubt, referees should call for a timeout. If a towel flies into the ring he should signal timeout in order to determine the source of the towel or to throw it out. The referee is not only the arbitrator, he also has to be the regulator when someone else creates a problem, such as a mismatch. He then has to clean it up, especially during a televised fight. He then has to put an end to it and move on to the next match.

The referee has several responsibilities and perspectives, and since every fight is different, he has to sort them out in the order of their importance or their priorities: To enforce the rules, are the fans important, and, do new fighters require special care? If a referee stops the fight too late a boxer might get hurt: if he stops the fight too soon, the fighter might not learn that the fight game can be highly unforgiving.

The referee could do a better job of regulating the flow of the show if he could use the one-minute rest period between rounds. That time is not available to him because he has to run around the ring collecting scorecards. As I mentioned earlier, at most matches, the referee has to admonish behavior, usually a fighter's or his trainer's. Adequate personnel management suggests that admonishment is more effective if it is conducted in private. Then, the best time to talk to the corner folks would be during the one-minute rest period between rounds, because the fans can't hear conversations in the ring, and are not looking at the ring activities during that time. This is another reason why the scoring should be conducted electronically, because the referee needs that time to better regulate the flow of the contest.

In the first chapter, I said that I have worked approximately 3,110 fights, keeping my own score in every contest I refereed. When it comes to a knock-down in a fight, the rules are very clear: "In the event of a knockdown the referee shall count to ten." Interestingly, these rules do not address the welfare, health or safety of the contestants. With that in mind, the doctor assigned to a fight cannot jump into the ring to determine if a boxer is dead or alive. The ring doctor serves at the pleasure of the referee. He may call the doctor if he wishes. The referee should always use the ring doctor, especially when he is not sure of the extent of an injury. Referees need to be safe because it only takes a minute or two for the doctor to check a contestant out. Doctors should always be allowed to determine if a fight can continue or should be stopped.

Agility is fundamental in the role of a referee. He must teach his legs that they must never stop moving during the contest, unless he has something to do, such as breaking the fight or talking to the fighters. When the referee stops moving, he obstructs somebody's view. If he stops moving and is close to the fighters, he will obstruct the view of many spectators; if he stops when he is far from the fighters, the obstruction of the view is fewer in numbers. If the referee moves like a jumping jack or faster than a roadrunner, he will be a distraction. The referee must always remember that the fans come to see a fight, not a clown that's always meddling, interfering, shouting, or performing gyrations with his arms.

Referees must always allow the bell to signal the start and end of all the rounds. They must never demand instant compliance. When they do that they are disrupting the train of thought and concentration of the fighters. Referees always need to be patient and allow the conditioned reflex to kick in. The third man in the ring should get close enough to both fighters so they can hear when he talks to them. Referees should allow their actions to acknowledge his comments. On numerous occasions it will be necessary for him to touch one or both fighters. Sometimes the touch will not be gentle, especially when the fighters are unable to hear him because their brains are locked-in on the business at hand; it's called concentration. The fighters know why they are in the ring, and when the referee steps out of the way they will usually resume the fight.

Effective communication is very important. When a boxer speaks a different language other than English, the referee must be extra careful because he will not understand when the fighter, for instance, complains about an injury or being hurt. Professional boxers do not quit, so when they complain about an injury, it's time to call in the ring doctor. In Las Vegas, Nevada, during a fight, one boxer was forced to continue fighting after he complained to the referee that he was hurt. That evening the fighter died because the referee did not understand Spanish.

Another very important aspect of the referee's job is that he must train himself to estimate the duration of the three-minute and one-minute periods, so that he has a good idea of when a round is coming to the end, as well as the end of the one-minute rest period. When the action is fierce, the fan noise exceeds the noise level of the bell, making it very difficult to hear its sound. When that occurs, the referee has to start watching the timekeeper, who will signal the ten-second warning, which is a different sound whether done with a whistle or a horn, or the sound of a hammer hitting the table. When the timekeeper sees that the referee can't hear that warning, or if the referee tells him that he can't hear the warning, the timekeeper can signal by slapping the canvas with his open hand. Before the fight begins, the referee should review with the timekeeper the different types of signal equipment he'll use, as he is the person in charge of starting and stopping the action in the ring.

Since the referee coordinates the team effort, he must constantly talk to everyone at the ringside, just to make sure that the timekeeper, the judge, the doctor and the inspectors feel that they are a part of the team. When something goes wrong, they help each other and correct a problem without anybody knowing that something was wrong. If someone screws up or something else goes wrong, the situation will reflect on the entire team.

CONCUSSIONS

During the progress of the fight, the referee must always be cognizant of a possible concussion or a stroke. Any type of change in the behavior of one of the fighters might be an indication that something is physically wrong with that boxer. "Every fight is the most important fight of my life," is the creed of every boxer when he jumps into the ring. Intense concentration is paramount in any competitive endeavor when an athlete expects to be victorious. When a match is for a world title and it is being televised, the boxing fans will generate the magnetism and excitement that will demand the referee's highest performance level. This type of scenario is a fairly common occurrence. It is highly possible in situations such as this where the ring doctor may not be at his station at the ringside, so what must the referee do? He finds himself in the middle of the biggest and best fight of the year, so he needs to give the timekeeper the time-out signal, send the one boxer to a far corner, then corner the other fighter and ask him to do three simple things: smile, speak a simple sentence, and to raise both arms. If the boxer has trouble doing any of these tasks, the referee must immediately stop the contest.

If there is a new sign of a possible stroke, referees should ask the boxer to stick out his tongue. If the tongue is crooked or if it goes to one side or the other, that can also be an indication of a stroke. If the ring doctor intervenes, he will handle the boxer's condition. When a fighter is knocked out or is suffering from a concussion, he will not be aware of that fact. He becomes aware of what has occurred when he is told about it afterwards: "You were knocked out," "you lost it," "you were beaten," "you were knocked down," and so forth. All of these types of changes are indications that it's time to call timeout and to bring in the ring doctor.

Dr. Javier Cardenas, of the Barrow Neurological Institute, says that a concussion is the mildest form of traumatic brain injuries, and that over 90 percent occur without people being knocked out. He adds that a concussion is serious but usually non-life-threatening if recognized, treated and given sufficient time to heal. About 95 percent of the people that suffer a concussion recover completely. Death is rare, usually occurring only in those who suffer a second head injury before healing from the first one. Here are some symptoms:

- Physical symptoms include headache, altered sleep patterns, dizziness, change in smell or taste, fuzzy or blurred vision, fatigue and sensitivity to light or noise.

- Behavioral symptoms include becoming very inhibited or very impulsive, and displaying mood swings, depression or nervousness.

- Cognitive symptoms include an inability to concentrate and difficulty reading, finding words or doing other things.

In the second fight between Evander Holyfield and Mike Tyson—for the World Boxing Association heavyweight championship, and held on June 28, 1997 at the MGM Grand Garden Arena in Las Vegas, Nevada—Tyson was fined for the second bite, not the first bite. That fight should have been stopped by referee Mills Lane after the first bite, and both boxers taken to the hospital. Tyson was suffering from a concussion and Holyfield was badly wounded. Everybody at the ringside, his trainer, the ring doctor and the commissioners fell asleep. Holyfield should have been taken to the hospital to have a piece of his right ear reattached—after Tyson bit him and detached a one-inch piece of cartilage from the top of the ear—and "Iron Mike" for observation and treatment for the concussion.

Another good fight to learn from was the Andrew Golota vs. Mike Mollo match, held on January 19, 2008 at the Madison Square Garden in New York City. From the fifth round on Mollo was suffering from a concussion. For seven rounds, "Merciless" was unconscious, swinging up and down from the knees to the back of the head of Golota in desperation, grabbing and holding, a complete foul the entire time. Golota's left eye was closed for the last four rounds, therefore "Powerful Pole" could not see Mollo's face or his right hand during those rounds. Needless to say, Golota won the WBA Fedalatin Heavyweight title by unanimous decision after 12 rounds.

As I have stated before, professional fighters do not quit. They sign a contract that states that they will fight, and they usually do. Quitting or dancing is considered a foul, therefore referees should not allow this behavior. If a fighter indicates that he is hurt, the referee signals a timeout, and calls in the ring doctor to determine the seriousness of the stoppage, because the boxing fans will always honor his call. A referee's actions will affect everybody on the team, therefore, when in doubt, a referee must ask, but do it in a promptly manner. The third man in the ring should not hesitate; if he is unsure, he must call timeout in order to talk to someone about the matter.

The referee's clothing is also important, and it must not be a distraction. The colors white and black are not good because they create too much contrast. A better color is light blue for the shirt and light gray for the trousers.

Before every boxing match begins there is a gathering in the middle of the ring by the referee and the two boxers. Historically, it has been called the pre-fight instruction. The only meaningful reason for this ritual is so that the gladiators learn to recognize the voice of the referee, and to allow the media to focus and adjust their video, photo and sound equipment. At a time that two contenders are fighting the most important fight of their lives, they could care less about rules and warnings from the referee. At that moment they are mentally preparing their battle plan which is going to require intense concentration. The rules and all questions should be reviewed during the weigh-in ceremony, which is usually conducted the day before the fight.

Immediately at the end of a round, the referee has to collect the scorecards and deliver them to the Commission's representative at the ringside; he has sixty seconds to walk around collecting the cards and to return to his corner. If one of the judges is slow in producing his scorecards, the referee should put him on the end of his collection route to save time that he might need before the start of the following round. In any endeavor that requires two or more persons to do the job, one person has to know what's going on everywhere. In the ring the referee is completely in charge, and if he is not keeping his own score he is not completely informed, so he must know how to judge, and should always have his own scorecard.

Even Rounds

The Arizona Boxing Commission rules state that in the scoring process, even rounds are rare. Some officials disagree, and they will point fingers and make negative comments about a judge that believes in even rounds. Even rounds are common, especially in a poor fight. The cause for a poor fight is that the professional boxer is not paid to fight, he is paid to show up. Even if he doesn't fight he still gets paid at the end of the show. Some judges state that when they are uncertain who won a round, they will arbitrarily pick one fighter as the winner of that round, and when the next dubious round occurs they will award it to the other boxer. Hence the question arises: what happens if that second uncertain round does not materialize? Does the second gladiator get shortchanged? There's nothing wrong with an even round, yet there is something wrong with a judge who will steal a point from a gladiator to satisfy his own personal needs as a judge or his inability to differentiate an even round. Such judge is exaggerating and magnifying the importance of this job, as well as trying to glorify the act of judging. Ten points for a round is a reward for a boxer who performs in an outstanding manner, in the same fashion as applauding for a job well done. Poor judging is fine in a lousy boxing match. Dancing the rope-a-dope, running, showing off are all fouls in the Arizona rules. Lousy fights don't count in a good match. Score instantly. When the fan is happy, due to a good even battle by the two gladiators, both warriors must be rewarded equally with 10 points each.

PROFESSIONAL OR AMATEUR BOXING?

The Manny Pacquiao vs. Timothy Bradley welterweight title boxing match, held on June 9, 2012, at the MGM Grand Garden Arena in Paradise, Nevada was, in my opinion, an amateur fight, and was judged accordingly. I scored this fight in favor of Pacquiao 120 to 112. It appeared that the three judges in this match were scoring an amateur boxing match because Bradley was fighting like an amateur boxer, chasing flies all night, waving his left hand repeatedly, and occasionally touching his opponent's gloves. Waving the left hand is what won Bradley the fight after 12 rounds, because in amateur boxing waving the hand is important. Obviously this was a highly controversial split decision that gave the WBO Welterweight title to Bradley.

Amateur boxing is a liability to professional boxing because it does not teach the basic fundamentals of several things, fisticuffs being one of them and of principal importance. They do not teach that before a boxer swings he must be close enough to touch his opponent or he will miss. Consequently, when a fighter finds himself in a mental and emotional crisis, his mind usually goes blank. As I previously noted, when that occurs the boxer's subconscious survival instincts will protect him by reverting to the training he received in the gym; it's called the condition reflex. A hard punch is not a hard punch to every judge, therefore the hard punch must be qualified with a definition: a hard punch must visually affect the receiver of the blow or it's not a hard punch. Referees must review the chapter on judging a fight.

WHEN THINGS GO WRONG

The Victor Ortiz vs. Floyd Mayweather, Jr. championship WBC Welterweight title fight, held on September 17, 2011, at the MGM Grand in Las Vegas, is a good example of the things that can go wrong in any boxing match. The video and photographs of that match show the two fighters and the referee and need little to no explanation. The images speak for themselves, and reveal numerous things that can go wrong in a fight. It shows the reasons for routine factors and actions that the referee must follow during the course of every fight. It also exemplifies the fact that even highly-experienced officials will make mistakes which result from the fast-paced nature of a boxing match, and that the number of mistakes will diminish as the amount of experience of the official increases. These mistakes occur because there have never been two fights that were identical. When the referee needs to stop the action (just like in the Ortiz vs. Mayweather fight), he must follow a certain ritual as described below:

    - Look at the ring timekeeper and show him the proper timeout signal.

    - Look for the opponent (in this case it was Mayweather), and point to the corner where he wanted him to stay until he was finished with the defender (Ortiz).

    - After administering the discipline, he will then look for his opponent—who should still be in the corner where he was sent—and signal him to resume the fight.

During this highly controversial fight, Ortiz bumped Mayweather in the face with an intentional head-butt. Referee Joe Cortez immediately called timeout and deducted Ortiz a point for the foul, then motioned the fighters back together to continue the match. Mayweather caught

Ortiz off-guard with a left hook *before* both boxers were yet fully reengaged, and while the referee was looking away. Surprised by the punch, and still not raising his hands to resume the fight, Ortiz seemed to have briefly gazed at Cortez as if wondering why the referee didn't sanction Mayweather for that punch. Immediately after the first punch, Mayweather hit Ortiz once again with a flush right to the face, dropping Ortiz straight onto the canvas.

Millions of people were watching this championship fight; for that reason, a professional conduct of the highest order should have been honored. Cortez should have called in the ring doctor to first examine Mayweather. Some logical concerns were: Was Floyd suffering from a concussion; was he ill; was he of sound mind when he cold-cocked Ortiz? And then go tend to Ortiz, who was still on the canvas. So the question arises: should Mayweather have been disqualified for conduct unbecoming of a world champion, and then awarded the crown to Ortiz? When a referee needs to separate two fighters he should tap them on the shoulders with the open palms of his hands, and say the word "break" repeatedly until their actions acknowledge his instructions. When that occurs, then the referee steps in between the boxers to address the matter. If necessary, the referee should make a timeout signal. Referees must refrain from hollering from left-field "keep them up" or "watch your head." If the boxer hears the referee's chants, his train-of-thought has been disrupted, and he might get—as a result—a good whipping, especially if the referee didn't step in between them. By the way, the Nevada boxing director should not have allowed referee Cortez to retire; it's their loss since he is one of the best and experienced boxing referees in the world.

The prize ring can be a highly explosive place where crazy things can happen. Thus, the referee should never grab or hold the hands of the boxers because they might have to defend themselves. He can get in the way or between them as part of his job, and the risk of getting hit is always a possibility. In a case when the fight needs to be stopped in order to end a beating, referees should not turn their backs on the aggressor. If they do, they might receive a "rabbit punch"—a sharp chop with the edge of the hand to the back of the neck—that could result in very serious injuries. The atlas and the axis are the top two cervical vertebrae, they are the weakest point in the spine, and they form the joint connecting the skull and spine. A rabbit punch to that spot could kill or render a referee completely disabled. For that reason, he should not turn his back on a "war machine." If he needs to stop a beating, he must face the aggressor until he stops swinging and acknowledges his presence, before he tends to the fighter that is getting the whipping. When a fighter goes down hard, the referee must approach the downed fighter slowly in the event that he is spring-loaded and springs right up on his feet.

During the review of the rules, which should be conducted during the weigh-in ceremony, the boxers are told that they must protect themselves at all times. This does not mean exclusively during the contest; it means during the entire time they are in the ring. A good example of this is what occurred after the James Butler vs. Richard Grant fight, on November 23, 2001. At the end of the fight, when the decision was announced, Butler charged Grant and hit him with a hard right, knocking him down. Butler was tried and convicted for aggravated assault and served four months in a detention facility. During another fight between two women, a friend of one of them grabbed his friend from behind in an attempt to stop the fight, then the other woman pulled a knife and stabbed the one being held. Another crazy incident can be seen in a video on the YouTube channel. A corner man jumped into the ring during a fight, grabbed the opponent from behind and then his fighter started beating the boxer being held.

Referee's Concentration

All the boxing rule books fail to include a chapter on concentration. The chapter on the psychology of the mind is going to alter a few of our rules. One example is the discipline of a boxer during a match. The referee approaches the fighter and asks him if he heard him or is aware of the infraction. In the heat of the moment, the contestant will not tell a lie; if he says that he did not hear him it's credible, because he was concentrating on the fight. Immediately, the referee must make a decision, take action and then move on.

On one occasion, I was working a highly competitive match between two welterweight boxers. After several rounds, both gladiators were bleeding profusely and not showing signs of fatigue. In the middle of one of the rounds, I decided that one of these fighters was hurt excessively, so I jumped into the middle of them and stopped the fight. I then awarded the fight to the other fighter. The losing fighter was perplexed at my action, his corner complained loudly and his followers were highly upset. When the referee makes a decision like this, there is no turning back; he should stick to it. Of course, some of the fans will never forgive you, and that stoppage might haunt you for a long time. After that fight, Dr. McDougall (the ring doctor) told me that if that fight had continued, the loosing fighter would have sustained further injuries which might have ended his career, because his nose was badly broken.

The referee must learn to concentrate with such intensity that it will enable him to switch off and on all extraneous sounds that don't belong in the ring. This capability is essential for proper management of a fight that is in progress. In order to do a good job, the referee must blank out the television and photographer's cameras. If he poses for the cameras he is neglecting his job, and the cameras don't like this behavior.

The Arizona rules for boxing allude to the fact that the referee is in complete charge of all these rules. Nevertheless, the rules of the Association of Boxing Commissions (ABC) clearly state that the referee is the only person who has the authority to interpret fight rules. With that in mind, the rules exonerate the referee, especially if the referee is wrong or makes a mistake.

4

THE BOXING JUDGE
The Scorekeeper

Boxing is not a national sport, one that is limited to one country; it's a worldwide sport, in which the word "judge" is used by everybody, all over the globe. Other names that are synonymous with the word judge are: His Lordship, His Honor, chancellor, arbiter, arbitrator; they all settle disputes. Of course, during a boxing match, a judge is never called to settle disputes. He or she is never asked to adjudicate, to discuss the value of a blow nor asked about what he or she witnessed in the ring.

The decision of a boxing judge is cast in concrete, and is never overruled or changed. However, some decisions are discussed and criticized for eternity, some in poor light, others in favor of, but never overturned or changed. C.J. Ross—a female boxing judge—drew criticism for her scorecards in various high-profile matches. In one of these big fights in Las Vegas, Ross scored opposite the other two judges, and she was lampooned by the "experts." As a referee who worked and judged over 3,100 fights, I agreed with Ross. It appeared that the other two judges were scoring an amateur fight. This type of decision controversies are not uncommon or unusual, therefore, we must introduce change to the rules that will add professionalism to boxing. The word judge can remain in the rules, but it's fundamental to understand that the judge is not a judge *per se*, but rather a scorekeeper; a person who records the events that occurred... one round at a time.

To understand the importance of the boxing judge's job, we can use an example. Basketball players don't need courage to get on the court, all they need is a pair of very long legs. They are never in danger of getting hurt, all they need to do is run fast, very fast. But we know that in boxing the contenders require a lot of courage, because of the fact that the objective of the sport is to administer mayhem to an opponent. To be a successful professional boxer the individual must possess certain attributes: good health, high intelligence, agility, braveness, and have a state of mind that will enable him to successfully endure defeat (a whipping) while in the public eye. As I mentioned in a previous chapter, in every fight I had as a boxer I would always end up with a headache that would last two weeks. Therefore, an additional physical attribute that a world champion must possess is a very hard cranium, a skull that protects his brain.

Therefore, in return for being courageous, boxing judges shall award ten points to each warrior at the beginning of every round. In a round where both fighters give it hell, and as a result the scorekeeper does not instantly know which one won, the round turns into an even round, one in which both boxers get to keep all their ten points. In a round where one clearly outperforms his opponent, that opponent loses one point. In a round where one gladiator goes down from a blow, that boxer may lose two points. In a round in which one contender gets a thorough beating or goes down several times, he may lose three points, but never more than three. The rules state that a warrior can never lose more than three points, which means that the numbers in the scoring system, from zero to six, are never used.

In accordance to the rules, the referee has the authority to reprimand and deduct points for behavior unbecoming to a professional athlete, an authority that also extends to the judge. It's important to remember that, while in the ring, the referee is always moving, therefore he does not have the same instant view of the fight as the three judges at the ringside have. Thus, the judge may deduct a point when the referee misses something. That occurrence can be major such as a low-blow, or something minor such as showboating (taunting, dropping the gloves, daring an opponent to throw a punch, or engaging in other risky behaviors).

The reason for deducting points must be real or the deduction is arbitrary. I stated in the previous chapter that some officials believe that an equal round seldom occurs, so they will arbitrarily select a winner of the round and rationalize their actions by imagining a future ring occurrence that would correct the imbalance they have created. When a tie occurs in a major sport, they all have a method or system that extends the duration of a contest until one is victorious. In a boxing match that ends in a draw, which can be broken by adding another round to the contest or if the trainer, with the approval of the boxer, decides that the purse shall be split, that will end the contest. The proposed open scoring method would also eliminate most of the draws, because both fighters would be aware of the official score before the last round, and consequently fight to the death in that last round.

There are several reasons that the judge must record the outcome of the round instantly after the sound of the bell. The instantly part is important because the referee has only sixty seconds to collect cards and to deliver them to someone at the ring side, so very quickly the referee's hand will appear in the scorekeeper's face, demanding the scorecard. This means that the judge does not have the luxury of time to contemplate his decision on the outcome of the action in the ring.

Another reason is expediency, because we are not aware of the value of the television time. The going value of a short commercial is $100,000, and in a recent fight the commercial carried a value of 4.5 million bucks. In a fight that goes the distance, it takes the officials an average of six minutes to tally and announce the score. Officials must be cognizant of the value of that television time and announce the score immediately after the end of the fight. With electronic scoring, referees can announce the score in seconds and not have to worry about the arithmetic on the scorecards, because the computer does it all.

THE REAL MEANING OF THE WORD "JUDGE"

In boxing, the word judge is out of place. A more appropriate title for the judge should be evaluator or observer one, observer two and observer three. The dictionary defines the word judge as one who presides in a court of law giving advice on matters of law and deciding on the punishment on guilty persons, or one asked to settle a disagreement or to criticize or blame someone. None of the above definitions fit the actual job description of boxing judges. The word judge connotes somehow, that he is the executioner, and that his job consists of awarding the gladiators ten points in a round when their performance is admirable, and less than ten points when they do not meet his expectations, it comes down to an attitude like this: "I am the expert on fisticuffs. Therefore, if your performance does not measure up to my expectations, I will not award you ten points in the round."

Ideally, the job description of the judge should read in the rules book as follows: "The duty of the fight judge is to record the events in the fight ring, as they occurred." The actual job of the boxing judge is to document the events as they occurred, no more, no less. When two boxers fight a good, hard battle that is close, the judge must award ten points to each fighter; it's a reward for doing what they agreed to do by signing a contract that states that they will fight. When they do they will earn their points. When both fighters are rated, it means that a draw in the contest is possible because they are both equally skilled, therefore a victory will be the function of which is in better condition, mentally or physically or both. Sometimes the tide will shift in the latter rounds, so even rounds at the beginning of a battle should not be unusual.

Basketball is a good example of what occurs when two equals compete. The score in a game stays within one point back and forth until the last second of the game; they don't run out of gas because the players are rotated when they get tired. The boxing judge must never contemplate his decision or flip a coin for the winner of the round: no what ifs, no later, no what happened in the past, or no what might occur in the future. The judge must always document the score one round at a time as if it's the only round in the fight, and record the events that occur; that's the judge's job.

Another term we also must consider is effective punching, which must be defined because in amateur boxing "chasing flies" is highly acceptable and means: "Stay away or I will hurt you." Therein, "chasing flies" has little to no value in the professional ring. The definition of effective punching should be: A punch that has a purpose and is part of the victory plan.

Since depth perception is highly essential for viewing a fight, the judge must have two good eyes. Therefore, a person who has only one good eye should never be assigned as a judge. Judging a battle requires strict concentration. Psychology 101 teaches that the act of concentration is not innate but instead a skill which has to be developed, and that it is impossible to concentrate on two different subjects at the same time. For that reason, the judge shall not be engaged in two different mental activities at the same moment. Judges cannot be talking and watching at the same moment, so they should isolate themselves from all distractions during the contest. This aspect can be evaluated by watching the television analyst during a fight. These fight commentators are paid to provide meaningless rhetoric, and they do not understand that they are not judging the fight because they are concentrating on their dialog. As a result, they are always on the wrong side of the verdict, and then they throttle the judges. That's the reason the boxing judge is not an honorable profession, because television experts have branded them as incompetent. The judge must be thoroughly familiar with the chapter on mental discipline in this book.

Other factors to be considered on the outcome of a round are: skills, conduct, defense, aggressiveness, behavior, and highly important is their conduct, good or bad. The skills of the gladiator are a cloud that even highly-experienced judges often miss. Take for instance a short boxer fighting a tall opponent. The tall boxer will have a huge advantage because of his reach; with his long arms he can slap the tar out of his opponent from the left field, especially if he is fast on his feet. Rocky Marciano (5' 11"), Mike Tyson (5' 10") and Manny Elias (height not available) are examples of very short boxers for their weight division. So how did it come about that these boxers achieved their greatness? Marciano had 49 fights and 43 knockouts, and Tyson had 58 fights and 44 knockouts. They had a very hard head and a very firm determination. A short contender has to get inside his opponent's reach before he is able to bang away, and he will not get in without getting hit, and getting hit very hard. Frequently, the short fighter will allow his opponent to hit him in order to sucker him into his reach, where he would lay a haymaker (a punch in which the arm is whipped sideways from the shoulder joint with minimal elbow bend) on him. Arizona boxer Manny Elias was also a very short person in the Bantamweight Division (115 pounds and up to 118 pounds). He fought the world champion to a draw. Elias told me that he would not throw punches until the top of his head touched his opponent's chest, and most of all Elias' fights that he won, went the distance. So therein lies the dilemma for the judge. If a judge recognizes the strategy of this short gladiator, does he score the same way that judges score a fight in the amateur ring or does he allow some leeway? A judge would certainly, or Marciano would have lost the six fights that went the distance, and Tyson would have lost 10 fights.

During the contest, the judge must evaluate in his mind the difference between the value of a hard right or a good hook, as compared to one jab or several jabs. A hook is performed when a boxer turns the core muscles and back, thereby swinging the arm, which is bent at an angle. A jab is a short, sharp punch with little windup that a boxer uses to soften up his opponent or distract him before throwing a bigger punch. The judge must ask himself if five or ten jabs are as good as one hard right or one hard hook. It would be difficult to set a standard where one says that one right equals five jabs or one hard jab equals two light jabs. A chart with that kind of a standard might be a good training tool, but it can't be used in a fight due to the time constraints, and the fact that some fights are complicated, very fast and must be evaluated and scored in just a matter of a few seconds after the sound of the ring bell.

Before we criticize the score of the judge, we have to be aware that the magnitude of the punch has never been defined. The meaning of a hard punch will be a function of who we are. A hard punch can have different meanings to three different judges. A judge that has never experienced a knockout or a knockdown will define that blow different than a person who has never experienced fisticuffs. And a female judge that has been on the receiving end of a beating, by a man, will think that the above experiences were pussycat blows, and so that might be the reason a blow that is viewed from three different angles can have three different values. A hard punch might merely stimulate the competitive spirit in the competitor, and then what? Any blow that touches the opponent must then have the same value unless it has a visible negative effect on the opponent. If Oscar hits Mike with his best left hook he will arouse the competitive spirit in Mike, therefore we can't call it a hard punch. An experienced fighter will allow his opponent to hit him a few times to sucker him in, so if a gladiator allows his opponent to hit him under those conditions, will he be penalized? Therefore, a hard blow must be defined as a blow that has a noticeable negative effect on his opponent, otherwise it's just like a jab. A fighter that is fighting a contender that's significantly taller has to get inside of his opponent in order to reach him, he, therefore, has to possess a very hard head and must be able to take what might look like a beating, when in fact it's only part of his plan. So where do we draw the line? In the school of judging, in order to stabilize the scoring system, we must again sufficiently define the words blow and hard blow: A hard blow is not a hard blow unless it staggers or visibly shakes the opponent.

Judges must record the results of a round as if they were working a one round fight. Record it instantly; there can be no doubt in the judge's mind who won the round. If the judge does not instantly award the score, it has to be an even round. All fights are multi-rounds in which the total accumulation of points determines who is victorious. Every round must be scored free from thoughts of what has occurred in the previous rounds or what might occur in the future rounds. There is nothing wrong with an even round; it might mean that both gladiators performed magnificently, blood all over the place, two knockdowns, and so forth. A round scored even indicates that both fighters deserved a score of ten. An even round is not demeaning; it can indicate that both fighters deserved a ten. If a judge is not sure of who won the round, he must not flip a coin to determine the winner. It's not necessary, there's no urgency to award or to deduct points because the other rounds in the fight, when added together, will rightly determine the outcome. The word "even" has been labeled as a negative action by judges that were asleep or are incompetent, which is terribly wrong.

The reason that we have no even-round judges is that they have been brainwashed with negative meaningless rhetoric by experienced judges who don't believe in an even round. These judges have created an image that connotes poor judging skills when an even round is called. They claim that the judge that scored the even round was asleep or is blind. An even round only tells the warriors that they need to do more or less of what they were doing; it's not the product of a lousy round. There's nothing wrong with giving a ten to two boxers who are bleeding and exhausted after slugging it out for three minutes. But it is wrong to flip a coin to determine which one will not get a ten. Three or four even rounds, in a multi-round fight will not adversely affect the outcome. It may only mean that the fans will get to see a rematch of another exciting battle.

The judge should never try to physically count the number of blows during a round. Since the force behind the blows is never the same, counting has to be strictly arbitrary, and a blow that misses will have little to no value in points. He must read the chapter on concentration in this book. This chapter will remind him that if he becomes a fan during a fight or has a favorite boxer in the ring he will not judge fairly, because he stopped concentrating on what was happening in the ring. Finally, the judge's scoring monitor should be set up so that the judge will score one round at a time. This system of one round scoring will eliminate arbitrary scores. All of the uncertainties and variables in our present scoring system will vanish if we practice transparency. The chapter on open scoring shows that we were on the right track using this system.

5

THE BOXING INSPECTOR

The Commission Boxing Inspector is the most important role in the organization. In between the shows he monitors the fight venues to determine if the buildings are large enough, well-lighted, and if the dressing rooms are adequate.

By visiting the gymnasiums where boxers train and workout, the inspector needs to know which fighters are in good condition and which are not, and whether they are serious about the sport or are not.

The role of the inspector is also responsible for regulating the official weighing of boxers before a fight. He verifies that the warriors have their licensing documents and physical exams. He also reviews the rules with the fighters and the referee.

On the day of the show he visits the dressing rooms, monitors the hand wrappings, checks that the fighters' equipment and clothing are adequate, reviews the schedule with all the boxers, and makes sure they know the time schedule for their appearance in the ring.

During the fight, the inspector is present at every corner watching the activities of the seconds—the helpers who assist boxers with treatment of injuries and offer advice after each round—during the fighter's rest period and the battles.

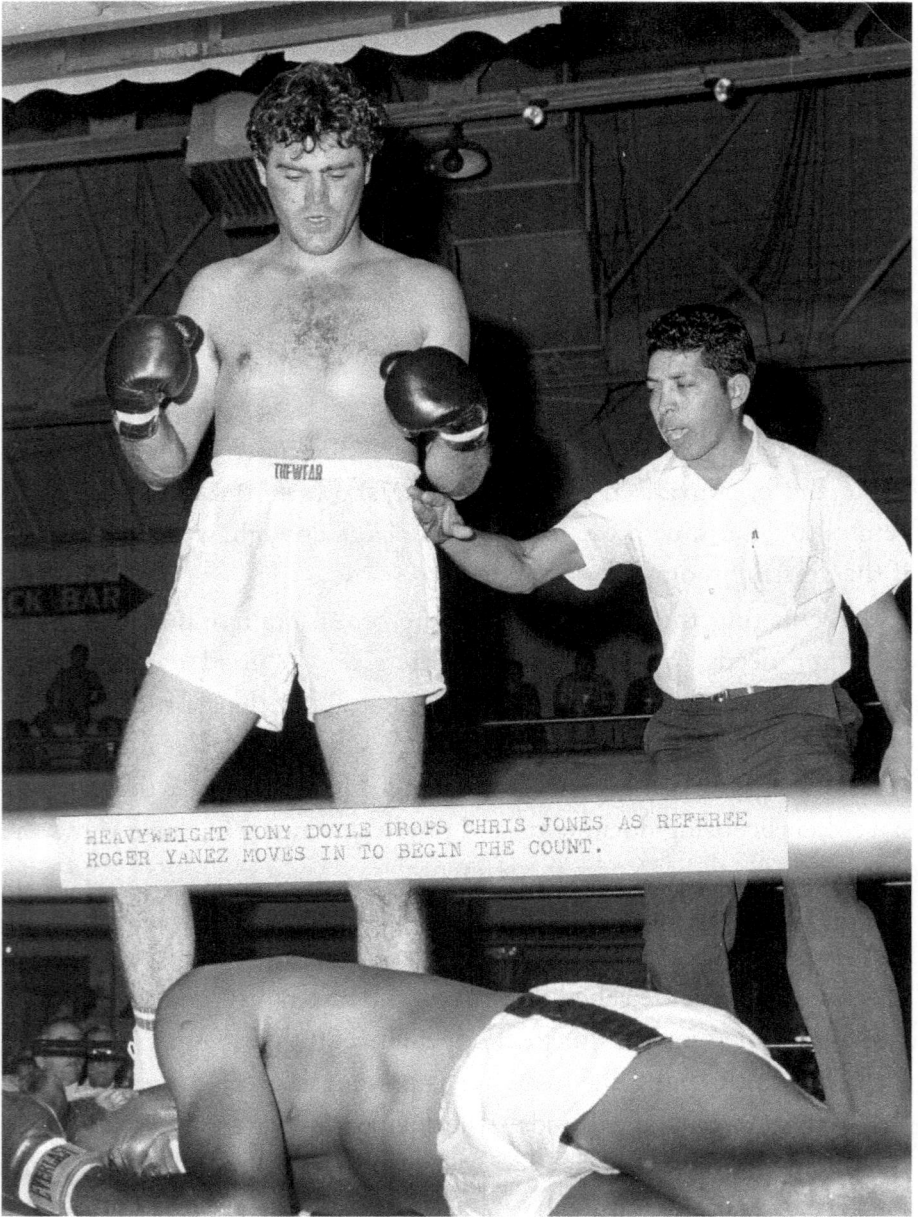

HEAVYWEIGHT TONY DOYLE DROPS CHRIS JONES AS REFEREE
ROGER YANEZ MOVES IN TO BEGIN THE COUNT.

Heavyweight Tony Doyle (standing) vs. Chris Jones (down). Referee
Roger Yanez moves in to begin the count. Circa 1968.

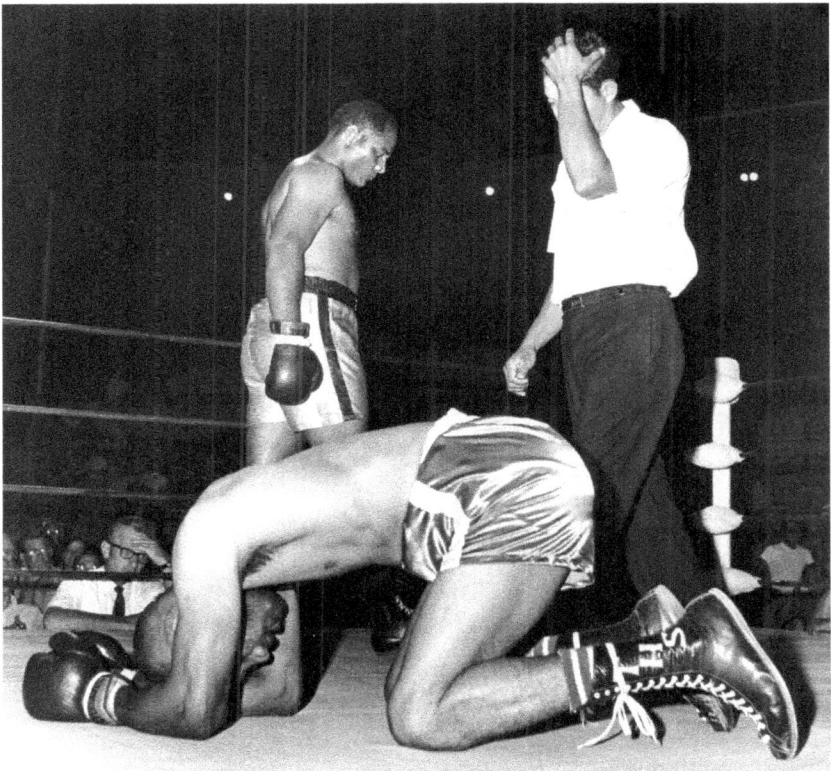

Ruben Castillo, 1996.

Referee Roger Yanez, circa 2003.

Jesus "El Martillo" Gonzalez vs. Nathan Martin at Dodge
Theatre in Phoenix, Arizona. December 5, 2003.

.. Continued from same fight as opposite page.

Yanez with boxer Michael Carbajal, circa 1992.

Yanez with boxer Becky Garcia and comedian Paul Rodriguez
at Dodge Theatre in Phoenix, Arizona. Circa 2004.

Yanez with boxer, circa 2003.

Below: Yanez with boxers, circa 1995.

ARIZONA STATE ATHLETIC COMMISSION

BILTMORE FASHION PARK
2454 E. CAMELBACK RD.
PHOENIX, ARIZONA 85016

JACK WILLIAMS
GOVERNOR

DR. ROBERT K. SHANNON
CHAIRMAN

MIKE QUIHUIS
COMMISSIONER

OTIS T. BURNS
COMMISSIONER

JAY EDSON
EXECUTIVE SECRETARY

13 September 1968

Mr. Roger Yanez
1624 W. Chipman Rd
Phoenix, Ariz 85041

Dear Roger:

In reply to your recent letter requesting the status of your three point
must scoring system by this Commission, please be advised that this
scoring method is in a state of inactivity since we are still awaiting
further elements of clarification from you concerning your recommendations for improving the mechanical operation of this system.

I again state that this scoring system of yours does have merit, but
there are many weak points in its physical operation. When you feel
you have the corrective measures made that will afford its use, please
bring these recommendations to the attention of this Commission, in
writing. Upon this receipt, I assure you that your scoring system,
with its recommendations will be most seriously considered by me
personally, as well as by the entire Commission.

Assuming that your recommendations will place this scoring system
before the Commission in its final form, after due consideration,
study, and deliberation, this Commission will then vote upon the
acceptance or rejection of this new scoring system.

My kind regards are enclosed to you and yours.

Sincerely,

R. K. SHANNON, Chairman

RKS:gb

No matter by what margin the loser is behind at the end of
the fight you will always hear, as it seems to be human nature,
by the seconds and the fighter we were robbed. As long as we
don't go to the round system I suggest that things remain in
the status quo.

May I be heard in person at the next meeting on these proposed
changed.

K. DONALD WREN
ATTORNEY AT LAW
XXXXXXXXXXXXXXXX
XXXXXXXXXXXXXXXX
PHOENIX, ARIZONA
1845 E. Ocotillo Rd.

February 1, 1967

Arizona State Athletic Commission
823 West Adams
Phoenix, Arizona, 85007

Attention: William Warren, Chairman

Gentlemen:

In reply to your letter suggesting comment on proposed changes
as outlined by referee Roger Yanez I wish to state I oppose the
two fold proposition.

The change from the ten point must system to the three point must
system would have the following disadvantages:

I.   If one contestant knows how far he is ahead he would slow
     up because he knew that if he held his opponent off he
     would be the winner.

II. If one of the contestants was knocked down twice in the same
     round and yet finished the round the spread of three points
     does not give enough latitude.

As to the other suggestion of announcing the points after each
round has many disadvantages and has been tried various times in
different states and then abandoned.

It must be remembered that a paying fight fan is the pay master
of this entire sport. It takes from him, that is the fan the
suspence which is really a climax when the final decision is
announced. Have you not seen the crowd around the ring awaiting
the announcer to give the final decision of the main event? This
is their climax if the fans are informed by announcement of the
points it would take the excitement from the fan and if one contestant were far ahead you will see the fans walking out before the
bout has been completed.

While a bout is scored by points after each round we must look as
the fan looks at the contest as a whole.

E. V. THORNE CONSTRUCTION CO.
4313 NORTH 15TH AVENUE
PHOENIX 15, ARIZONA

MEMBER:
AMERICAN ASS'N. OF ENGINEERS
ILLUMINATING ENGR. SOCIETY

LICENSE NO. 15624
CRESTWOOD 4-1833

4. (cont'd). If a fighter does not want to fight, slap him with a suspension for a short while and make it stick in the States we are allied with. He'll Learn!!

5. I can repeat, the Fans "Love" all the yelling they do. They really want it that way. After it is all over, they go their way, and are good sports about it. You can never change their minds about their

E. V. THORNE CONSTRUCTION CO.
4313 NORTH 15TH AVENUE
PHOENIX 15, ARIZONA

MEMBER:
AMERICAN ASS'N. OF ENGINEERS
ILLUMINATING ENGR. SOCIETY

LICENSE NO. 15624
CRESTWOOD 4-1833

January 20, 1967

William Warren, Chairman
Arizona State Athletic Commission
Phoenix, Arizona

Dear Mr. Warren:

Regarding the recent receipt of request for review of the "Scoring" system for Boxing and the proposed "Three Point Must System", I wish to make the following comments.

It is my personal opinion, that the proposed system would NOT make any difference in the attitude of the fighters themselves. Frankly, I believe it would add to more confusion.

Having been a Boxing Judge here for years; also participating in the same in the Army when called upon and also actively participating in Boxing on a College team in Inter-Collegiate sports, I feel I can render a fairly decent opinion and decision.

1. Judges and Referees should be well experienced in this sense. Judging by all concerned should never be rendered on a "Hometown Boy" basis or for any other reason than good sportsmanship, aggressivness and being the better boxer in that particular bout.

2. The "Point Must System" - whether it be 10 or 3 point is still the same, with the exception of just doing a little more mathematics in totaling. Very seldom are 7 points given to a loser of a round, unless he has been knocked down and was absolutely helpless for the balance of that round. If he gets up and makes a good "comeback" he will probably get a "10-9 or a 10-8" round. Check the old cards and see if that isn't true!!

3. In announcing the score at the end of each round, I agree it would be a novel idea, however I would say it would add to much confusion. Instead of "Noise" at the end of the bout, we will have it at the end of each round. Both the handlers and the fans, will still go for their favorite and that is something we cannot change by a point or any other system. People being people, is something we cannot change again from yelling "We Wuz Robbed". And beside it is all part of the game!!

4. There is nothing wrong with a "Draw" decision being rendered. I have been involved in very few draw decisions. It can be very readily seen that from opposite sides of the ring, different aspects of the fight are seen, and it wouldn't be fair to any fighter to do otherwise than to "Call our Shots" as we see it.

LEE *Optical* OF ARIZONA, INC.

13 June 1967

Mr. William Warren
Arizona Athletic Commission
823 W. Adams St.
Phoenix, Arizona 85007

Dear Bill:

In keeping with our recent meeting in which it was mentioned
that it might prove advantageous for all concerned to have a
short memo made that would be handed out to each ticket
purchaser, that would briefly describe the new scoring system,
the following rough draft is submitted for your consideration:

Dear Boxing Fan:

By public request, we will use a new method of scoring
tonight, and are requesting your opinion of this system.

In brief, this new system, which will be used for the
UNDERCARD bouts only, consists of making known
to all the winner of each round as shown by the total
of the point score cards of the judges and referee, at
the end of each individual round. The boxer with the
highest sum total at the end of the bout, as in the past,
will be declared the winner.

To help us to further determine the merits of this new
scoring system, we request your cooperation. Please
note your opinion, in the area shown on this card, and
deposit this in one of the large (blue) boxes located at
each exit.

Thank you,
Arizona Athletic Commission

☐   YES -- I like this new scoring system.
☐   NO--- I do not like this new scoring system.
(Please check only one)

Cordially,

Bob

R. K. Shannon
RKS:mj

LEE OPTICAL OF ARIZONA, INCORPORATED ● DISPENSING OPTICIANS
EXECUTIVE OFFICES   ●   P. O. BOX 2920, PHOENIX, ARIZONA 85002

Arizona State Athletic Commission
Page 2
January 21, 1967

     3. On the other hand, a judge sitting
in his particular spot, and seeing the fight from
his angle, hearing the scores at the end of each
round, and realizing that his scoring was, some if
not vastly, different from the other judges, might
be influenced by the other judges' decision.
This would in turn eliminate the very purpose or
reason for which judges sit on different sides of
the ring.

     These are the three principal defects to

ょ

STEPHEN W. CONNORS
ATTORNEY AT LAW
SUITE 810 LUHRS TOWER
JEFFERSON AT FIRST AVENUE
PHOENIX, ARIZONA 85003
———
TELEPHONE 258-5726

January 23, 1967

Arizona State Athletic Commission
823 West Adams
Phoenix, Arizona 85007

Attention: William Warren, Chairman

Dear Bill:

     I have given quite a bit of thought to
the proposed Three Point Must scoring system
advocated by Referee Roger Yanez. Roger is to
be complimented and commended for the thought he
has given this matter and the time expended outlining the method of scoring.

     I should like however to go on record
as being opposed to the proposed scoring system.
First of all, such a system is not used by any
Boxing Commission in the world. This is true
possibly for some of the following reasons:

     1. Score cards are now added and checked
at the end of each fight. Even then occasionally
error creeps in. If said score cards were gathered
and added at the end of each round, you multiply
the possibility of error by the number of rounds
of the fight. In other words, in a ten-round fight
there are ten times as many chances for error, and
in a fifteen round fight fifteen times as many
chances for error as under the present system.

     2. Roger points out that sometimes a
new judge lacking experience does not see the
fight as do the more experienced judges. If on
the illustration, Judge 3, referred to as the third
judge of the Smith-Jones fight, is the new judge,
then his error is magnified and Jones would be the
winner of the fight by a considerable margin in
spite of the fact that two out of three, and at that
the two more experienced judges, saw the fight a
draw.

*The main opposition to scoring on total points, as suggested,
would be that it would be possible to nullify the scorecard of one
or of two of the officials by total points on the third official's
card . The reason for three officials is to allow two of them to
determine a winner. If the result is scored on total points accumulated by all officials, it would be possible to inherently override
an individual judge's rating of the fight.*

*I do think the Commission should adopt the California rule on
a "technical draw." This is interpreted as in the case of a fighter*

815 Litchfield Rd.,
Goodyear, Arizona
January 29, 1967

Chairman
Arizona State Athletic Commission
823 W. Adams,
Phoenix, Arizona

Dear Mr. Warren:

In regards to your correspondence of January 14 meeting and
proposition of scoring changes submitted by Referee Roger Yanez,
I offer the following opinion.

In my years of experience, I have very seldom been approached
by a participant or his handlers claiming that they have been vic-
timized by the official's decision.

Secondly, as a trainer, coach and referee, I have rarely en-
countered a fighter's advisors who would tell him to ease up if he
was ahead on points. I believe wholeheartedly and concur fully with
Mr. Yanez that any sport, and particularly boxing, should be a dynamic sport rather than a static one. If the means of making this
sport dynamic is by changing the scoring system, then by all means
do so.

I have seen the score announced at the end of each round in one
instance only. This was at San Jose State College in 1949-50, where
the scoring by officials was flashed on a lighted scoreboard for all
fans to see. This proved unsatisfactory evidently, as it was dis-
continued the following year. It did tend to create animosity after
each round, at a particular official, rather than initiating the in-
centive desired.

I believe the poorer fights result from a lack of ability and
conditioning of the fighters, or from a poor selection and matching
of the participants, rather than one fighter "easing" off because he
is ahead on points.

The present ten point must scoring system allows for seven points
to the fighter who is knocked down once; six points for two knockdowns,
and so on, depending on his comeback or lack of it during the remainder
of the round.

My suggestions would be to either adopt the New York system of
scoring by rounds, which allows for an alternate one point per round
score in case of a draw, or by the California five point must system.
Then , if it seems advisable, try announcing the round score at the end
of each round and see how it is received by the fans and member of the
sport.

June 3, 1967

We, the under signed, as boxing fans
hereby recommend to the st...
try, on a trial...

200 Signatures

We, the under signed, as boxing fans and boxing enthusiastes
hereby recommend to the State Atheletic Commission that it
try, on a trial basis at your discretion in one of the near
future boxing cards; The Yanez Method of Scoring Boxing Contests.
In an effort to find a solution that will put the sport
of boxing back on the road to success.

Name	Address
Emilio Martinez	4316 W. Crittenden Ln.
Hector O. Martinez	2119 W. Grant St.
Jr R. Garza	6240 S. 1 Ave
Michael Ruiz	6426 S 6th Ave
Raymond Betancourt	1630 W Chipman Rd.
Felix C Novena	817 W 5th Way
Jr. O. Como	901 E Vineyard
Clinton Warren	1439 E Culver.
Macedonio Sandoval	3307 N. 38 Dr.
Ralph M. Gutierrez	3233 W. Roosevelt
Raymond Gipp	4032 W. Krall St.
Paul E. Gonzalo	1247 E. Grant St.
E.J. Dobson X	2742 W Pierce St.
Eddie R. Ines	5640 S. 3rd St
Antonio J Diaz	2135 E Lincoln St.
P.B. Renteria	1223 N. Oakleaf Dr.
Enrique V. Garcia	3336 E. McKinley St.
Mike Korin	2519 N. 40th Ave
Augustin Ramirez	2064 W. Chambers
James J. Hart	2437 E. Marilyn Rd.
Rudy Pineda	2731 W Belleview
Ralph C Garrels	2942 N. 47th
Carlos Sanchez	2328 N 29 Pl
Jean A. Elliot	3318 W Culver
Pete Perez	5484 ...

Sportatorium

1717 E. McDOWELL RD.   PHOENIX, ARIZONA

ARIZONA SPORTS ENTERPRISES, INC.   WRESTLING PROMOTIONS, INC.
258-8981   258-9528

Jan. 26, 1967

Mr. Wm. Warren
Chairman
Arizona Athletic Commission
Phoenix,Ariz.

Dear Mr. Warren:

I received your letter and recommendation concerning
a scoring and plan to announce scores between rounds.

I won't go into a long explanation as to my reasons,
but I strenously oppose the scoring recommendation as
well as the idea of announcing the score between rounds.

Being the most active person in boxing hereabouts, and with
long experience in boxing, I take exception at the
attempts of persons with little experience and small
ability in this field to bring forth such things as this
with little merit. I mean no offense to Mr. Yanez in any
way. He isn't alone in such matters.

I do hope before such ideas are adopted, everyone will be
given a chance to be heard, expecially those active in
the promotion, training and activity of boxing.

Always the best to you and the members of the commission,
I remain,

Your's in sport,

Al Fenn

PS The members of the commission are my guests at the
closed circuit showing of the Clay-Terrell fight
Feb. 6 at Madison Square Garden. Tickets will be
sent to you.

★ BOXING   ★ WRESTLING   ★ HIGH BANKED SKATING   ★ AUTO RACING

page 2-

I do know that the State laws call for a 3-man commission
plus the Secretary, and if you and your group plan to accept
applications for one- please keep me in mind.

I served from 1958 until 1962, and would have remained, but
due to much travel on my permanent job, I felt it best to resign.

Now that I am back in the Valley, I would be pleased to get
back into the local activity, and it would, in no way interfere
with my job as Executive Secretary of the World Boxing Assoc.,

WORLD BOXING ASSOCIATION

from the
OFFICE OF THE EXECUTIVE SECRETARY

JAY EDSON
1369 EAST OREGON
PHOENIX, ARIZONA

PHONES — 272-1823 or 274-1498

June 7th, 1967

Robert Shannon, M.D.
State Athl. Comm.
Scottsdale, Arizona

Dear Dr. Shannon :

I have not had the pleasure of meeting you since your appoint-
ment to the Commission, but hope to do so in the near future.

I read with much interest today about the meeting set for
Tuscon on June 10th, and especially with reference to the item
of possibly changing the scoring system from a 10-point must
to a 3-point setup.

Please bear in mind, that as the first Executive Secretary of
the Arizona Commission in 1958, I was very involved along with
the Commissioners on the matter of the scoring, and writing the
rules as well. At that time the WBA(of which Arizona was then,
and is now a member) used the 10-point must, but now uses the
5-point must, which is generally accepted all over the world.

Why Roger Yanez feels a 3 point system is best, is unknown to
me. He is a fine official and I am sure has some good reasons
for it, but I want you and your group to know that if you pass
this proposal, Arizona shall be the only State in the entire
world who uses anything less than a 5-point system. Not that
any state or country has to use a special system, but it is
generally assumed that all WBA member states go along with the
same scoring system. As for the idea of turning in the score
cards at the conclusion of each round----I agree that this has
much merit.

I hope you do not mind my contacting you like this, but ,after
all, we are interested in the furtherence of good boxing, and
I would be happy to assist wherever possible. By the way- after
5 years as Arizona Exec.Secretary, I feel that I am very qualified
in that position, and understand that the spot is vacant now due to
Mr. Pena being involved in the State legislature.

BUILDING BETTER BOY'S FOR MANHOOD

PHOENIX

Boys Athletic League of Arizona, Inc.   *K*

1646 EAST WASHINGTON

PHOENIX, ARIZONA   Telephone 253-5461

ALEX M. FIMBREZ, President
JACK MORRISON, Vice-President

April 7, 1967

ADVISORY BOARD

FRANK FUENTES, Chaplain
American Legion, Post 44

Rt. Rev. JOSEPH M. HARTE
Bishop of the Diocese of Ariz.

MANUEL PENA, Jr.
State Athletic Commission

FRED C. STRUCKMEYER, Jr.
Vice-Chief Justice Supreme
Court of Arizona

Rabbi ALBERT PLOTKIN
Temple Beth Israel

JESSIE ALVIDAREZ

State Athletic Commission
823 W. Adams

Dear Chairman Warren:

Roger Yanez talked to me about a change that he has
proposed , to the Commission, for scoring of boxing.

I strongly recommend that the commission adapt this
change, for I have seen it work. In 1956 I had a
fight in Florida where a system similar to this one
was used.

The score was being posted after each round. At the
end of the 4th round I was very sure that I was way
ahead when my second told me that I was behind, The
score was three to one. My second then told me that
I could only win by a knockout. I then went after him
and knocked him out. If I had not known the score
at the end of the 4th round I might have lost that
fight.

At the end of that fight the audience really applauded.
I am sure they were applauding only the 5th round
because I stopped some good ones myself while going
for the knockout.

Respectfully yours,

Alex M. Fimbrez

Dear Boxing Fan:

By public request, we will use a new method of scoring tonight, and are requesting
your opinion of this system.

In brief, this new system, which will be used for the UNDERCARD bouts only, consists of three changes as follows: (1) Scoring will be based on 0 to 3 points.
(2) In-between-rounds rest period will be 1½ minute. (3) Scores will be
announced at the end of each round. The boxer with the highest sum total at the
end of the bout, as in the past, will be declared the winner.

To help us to further determine the merits of this new scoring system, we request
your cooperation. Please note your opinion, in the area shown on this card, and
deposit this in one of the large boxes located at each exit.

Thank you,
ARIZONA ATHLETIC COMMISSION

Yes----I like this new scoring system.

No------I do not like this new scoring system.

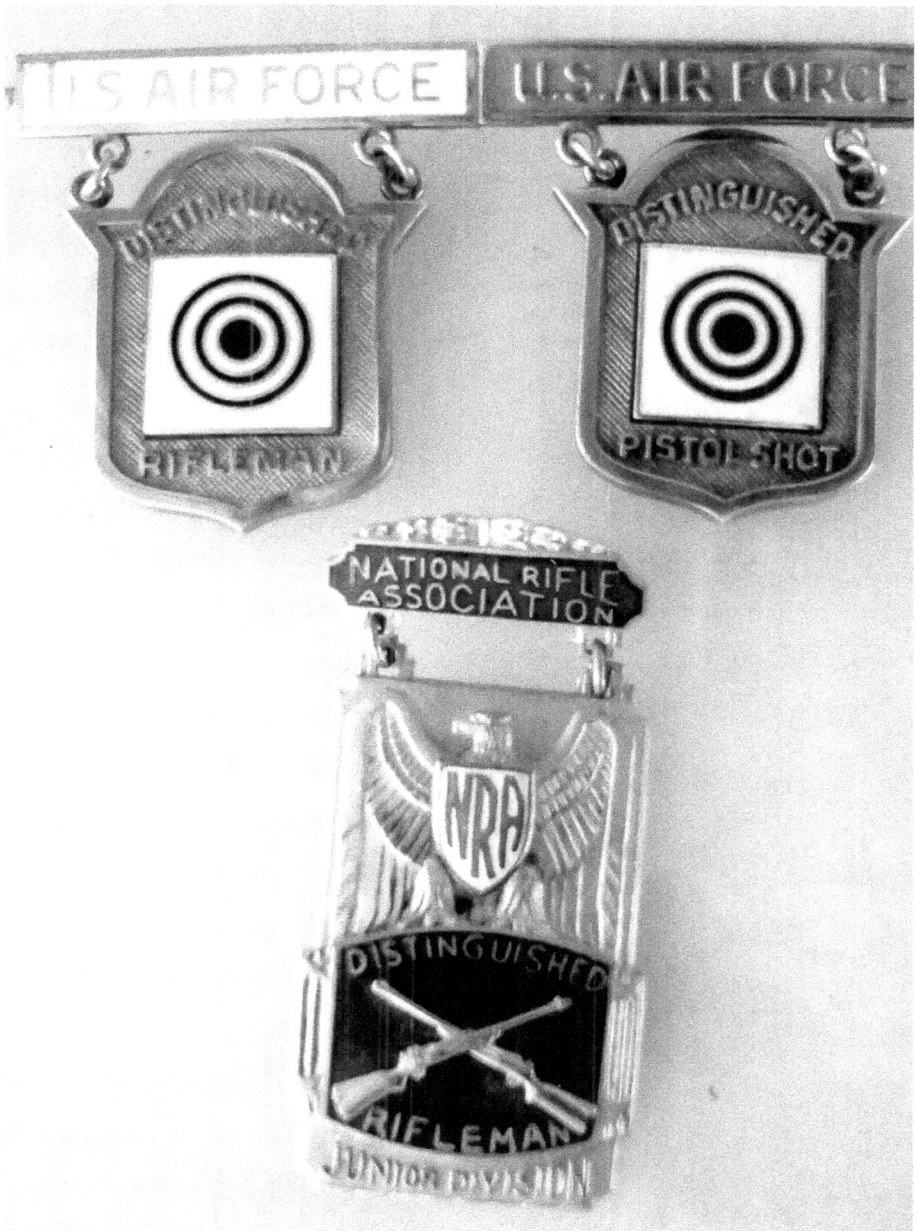

Distinguished Badges: Top left is the Rifle Badge No. 213; top right is the Pistol Shot Badge No. 193; and, bottom Smallbore Badge with the .22 rifle.

From left to right: Yanez, Jones, and Jenson, circa 1955.

Left: Yanez with a 120 MM shell and powder weighing 100 pounds used as an ack-ack. Circa 1953. Right: Yanez and George Horvath (a survivor of the USS Indianapolis on a refueling mission out of Phoenix on the KC-135 in 1985).

Left: Yanez and Charles Cano, circa 1985.

Below: Col. Louis Olivas, circa 1985.

Both Olivas and Cano could hit a bottle cap (the size of the target bullseye) ten times at 50 yards with a 45 caliber automatic pistol.

6

MENTAL DISCIPLINE

T he purpose of this chapter is to acquaint those in the sport of boxing with the need for mental control processes, and the development of their attention and concentration span during the course of a match, whether they are officials or boxers.

Nobody knows the source of the act of concentrating. We all know that it exists but we don't understand how, why or where it comes from. In this chapter you'll learn how to develop the ability to concentrate.

In most sports—football, baseball, basketball, tennis and even golf—one can see concentration in action. In baseball, former professional baseball left fielder Barry Bonds was suspected of using steroids to maintain his hitting success. I disagree that he mastered the act of concentration. Professional golfer Tiger Woods "has it," or had it at one time, it wants to surface and maybe it will. However, when he turns 50 years old, he will be moved into senior golf where he will "die a slow death."

The capacity of the brain does not diminish as one gets older. Dr. Joel D. Wallach—a veterinarian and naturopathic physician—says that when a person dies of old age he or she dies from malnutrition, because the person was not getting the vitamins and minerals all human beings need. Therefore, for sure and for certain, if we provide the above needs for the brain, our brain's capacity will not diminish because the brain is just another part of the human anatomy that will properly function if we take good care of it.

In the sport of golf there is the belief that at a certain age a golfer's brain capacity diminishes, therefore the golfer will then have to play with the old folks. I say no! When we watch an athlete on the tube we are able to tell, by his or her demeanor and facial expression, if he or she is concentrating or not concentrating, and therefore if such athlete will prevail or loose a competition. Most athletes are not aware that they are losing it; their performance tells them they are finished, so they just give up. If they understand that the power of concentration is an attribute, a physical function that requires simple exercises, they will be able to persevere until age 80 and not die at age 40.

Competitive marksmanship, both pistol and rifle, is the only discipline that fully understands that the act of concentrating is not innate but rather a skill that must be developed. That fact was perpetuated by the Germans and the Swiss. They were the first to advance that hypothesis, when they combined medicine, physiology and athletics, and as a result, they have monopolized the winner's podium in most of the competitive shooting events.

In boxing there have been several fighters who understood concentration. Former professional boxer and two-time world heavyweight champion George Foreman is one of them. In his November 5, 1994 fight with Michael Moorer—billed as "One for the Ages"—he was told by his corner that he had to build up points or that he would lose the battle. Foreman, who was 45 at the time of this fight, told his corner that he would wait until his opponent (26 at the time) lost his concentration, and at that time he would nail him, and he did. Nicaraguan professional boxer and three-weight world champion Alexis Argüello also understood the act of concentration. He would wait until the last two rounds and then go after his opponent.

In sports we hear the word "focused," which is often used synonymously with "concentrated," in order to designate a state of effortless absorption which usually accompanies moments of sporting excellence. Accordingly, sport psychologists state that the ability to concentrate effectively is a vital prerequisite for a successful performance. One must develop a ritual that will lead to the act of intense observation along with the desired endurance. The ritual must be simple and is usually subconscious.

The referee's job is a little different. He must focus on everything in and outside of the ring, and on anything that might interfere with the flow of the fight. When the fight is being televised, the referee must block out the TV from his mind. The people come to see a fight, not a clown. The media can tell when one poses or worries about being seen or not being seen on the television, and they don't like it. If what happened is not what you want happening you were not concentrating, "pure and simple."

The key to the top of any competitive endeavor is the ability to concentrate. The ability to concentrate is critically important and highly essential, and without it one will never experience the ultimate objective. Mental control and mental endurance are highly essential in a boxing match as a judge or a fighter, and one should be thoroughly schooled on the impact that the power of concentrating has on the individual's performance. "Why did you miss? Why did you not hit? Why did you not see?" These are never-ending questions that we have all heard. "I wasn't concentrating," is always the response. "If you weren't concentrating why did you step up... dummy?" So here lies the solution to a dilemma which has perplexed us forever.

A simple definition of the word concentrate does not exist, so let's talk about it. First of all, psychology experts will tell you that the ability to concentrate is not innate, that it's a skill that one must nurture. That the ability of the brain to concentrate is like a muscle; it will grow or shrivel depending on the amount of use it gets. Repeated practice will solidify the traits necessary to develop the mind's ability to control the essential mental processes.

The military marksmanship manual states that it's physically impossible for the mind to think about two different things at the same time, that the mind bounces back and forth at a very fast pace. Therefore it takes a lot of practice to teach it how to stand still and concentrate exclusively on one single subject. This all means that during a fight, if the fighter can hear his trainer yelling instructions or the crowd screaming or a clown in the ring that's also yelling "stop; box; watch your head," his mind is not on the business at hand and he will, therefore and without a doubt, get a good whipping.

The truth about the act of concentration is self-evident and omnipresent. In a previous chapter, I mentioned my friend Mr. Mac. He was 90 years of age when he was still hiking into the Grand Canyon, by himself, and still working eight hours a day at his law practice; his age did not slow him down.

The senior golfers—players aged 50 and above—believe that age forbids them to compete with younger players like Woods (1975), but they should not allow anyone to push them into the ancient's group. These and other factors have managed to interfere with our ability to adequately disseminate reality from myth, and to understand that the full meaning of the word concentrate has no bearing on one's age.

In his book "The Psychology of Concentration in Sport Performers: A Cognitive Analysis," Dr. Aidan Moran states: "The capacity to 'concentrate' effectively, or to exert mental effort on the specific task at hand while ignoring distractions, is widely regarded by athletes, coaches and psychologists as the key to successful performance in competitive sport." He also states that the word "focused" is often used synonymously with "concentrate" to designate a state of effortless absorption which usually accompanies moments of sporting excellence.

In 1984, Daniel S. Kirschenbaum claimed that competitive sports are almost entirely an exercise in cognitive and behavioral self-excellence.

The following scenario describes the power of the word "concentrate": I'm in the desert with a companion on a bird hunt. I am carrying the shotgun. My friend Bernie is a little behind me and to my right. In front of us a bird takes off, I aim the shotgun at the bird; it climbs and then banks to the right. I fire and the bird floats to the ground. I did not hear the loud explosion of the shot and I didn't feel the recoil of the shotgun. However, Bernie, who was not wearing hearing protection and was not concentrating on the bird or the explosion of the shot, received permanent damage to his eardrums. I was concentrating on the bird, therefore the noise and the kick of the rifle did not bother me. If I had felt the kick and heard the sound of the shot I would have missed the bird. By the same token, a boxer that is being chased by a big contender should not be able to hear a dumb referee yelling instructions. Duane B. Ford, a boxing judge and member of the International Professional Ring Officials (IPRO), says that he knows when he is concentrating when he does not notice the ring girls—the young ladies who carry a sign displaying the number of the upcoming round.

So, what exactly is "concentration"? Why do athletes often lose it? Paradoxically, at the very time they need it most. Can it be measured and improved? If so, how? Research shows that practicing with knowledge of results is one of the best ways of acquiring a skill, and that attention is a trainable skill. Accordingly, sport psychologists state that the ability to concentrate effectively is a vital prerequisite for a successful performance.

HERE ARE THREE EXAMPLES OF THE RITUAL
WE REFERRED TO ABOVE:

Baseball player Barry Bonds:

1. Step up to the plate
2. Plant both feet
3. Swing the bat twice
4. Bend your waist forward
5. Raise the bat
6. Look at the pitcher
7. Wait for the arm with the ball to begin the swing
8. Look for the ball

Golf player Tiger Woods

1. Step up to the spot that you like

2. Plant the golf ball on the ground

3. Look at the target

4. Estimate the range

5. Look at the golf ball

6. Hit the ball

Boxing judge:

1. Sit down on your chair

2. Straighten your back

3. Prepare your scorecard

4. Check your pencil

5. Look for the referee

6. Wait for the sound of the bell

In some states, the boxing referee is the third judge, which broadens his train of concentration. I said that the referee's job is a little different: he must focus on everything in and outside of the ring, and be aware of anything that might interfere with the flow of the fight. The referee must review his own ritual until he finds one that works. The ritual will develop into a skill that will produce the desired results. Referees must review it in their minds over and over. When the referee attempts it and it doesn't produce the desired results, he did something wrong. So referees must constantly talk to themselves: "What did I do that was wrong? Maybe a distraction of some kind?" With practice, referees will learn what to avoid as distractions.

The first fight between Manny Pacquiao vs. Timothy Bradley—on June 9, 2012, at the MGM Grand Garden Arena in Paradise, Nevada—is a classic example of the power or effect that the act of concentration has on the outcome of the fight. On this fight the experts were right, but that was an anomaly because they are on the wrong side far too frequently. They think they should never be wrong, so what do they do? They blame the boxing judge. As a result of their criticism, the professional boxing judge is not an honorable profession, because the experts have branded them as incompetent.

In the fight cited, Bradley won a highly controversial split decision to take the WBO Welterweight title which was a very close fight. Judges Duane Ford and C. J. Ross scored the fight 115–113 in favor of Bradley, while Jerry Roth scored the fight 115–113 in favor of Pacquiao.

Open scoring will prevent this type of controversy. It will eliminate the rope-a-dope exhibitions, and produce a huge battle by two gladiators, especially if the purse goes to the one who is victorious. It appears that Pacquiao and boxing promoter, founder and CEO of Top Rank Bob Arum, are the only persons who know what's going on. They setup a fighter that was basking in jail, since Floyd Mayweather Jr. served two months of a three-month sentence in a Las Vegas jail in 2012, in a misdemeanor domestic battery case. Prior to Floyd's "vacation" he had been dodging Pacquiao by saying that the Filipino boxer had to fight him for nothing (no pay). I believe that Pacquiao was afraid to fight a roadrunner that is faster than a speeding bullet, so he and Arum plotted against Floyd by blowing two fights to make Floyd think that Pacquiao was over the hill, therefore an offer by the Filipino of all-or-nothing, on the pay, would not be refused. All they had to do was allow Mayweather to get the purse that he wanted, but only if he was victorious.

Every six months the entire world experiences a change that affects everybody. If you doubt it just think back 50 years. We didn't have running water at home, we had an outhouse away from the house and down wind. No refrigerators either; we used an icebox. No coolers, no automatic transmissions. No jet planes; a trip to Hawaii would take ten hours in the propeller airplanes. The list is endless but just use your imagination: no false teeth, no bifocal lenses and on and on. But, why has professional boxing stagnated? We are on the same route as amateur boxing where the fans are the relatives of the gladiators. In the last one hundred years nothing has changed in boxing, why? In this book I offer two minor administrative changes that have been tried and they worked, but the time was not in the right century. I offer them again, and if they don't work we should try something else. We are in the entertainment business, therefore all professional boxers in the top ten of any of the ratings should be wealthy.

7

CONCUSSIONS

According to the federal agency Centers for Disease Control and Prevention (CDC), "a concussion is a type of traumatic brain injury—or TBI—caused by a bump, blow, or jolt to the head or by a hit to the body that causes the head and brain to move rapidly back and forth. This sudden movement can cause the brain to bounce around or twist in the skull, stretching and damaging the brain cells and creating chemical changes in the brain."

The American Association of Neurological Surgeons say 90 percent of boxers suffer some kind of brain injury while boxing, therefore boxing and concussions seem to go together.

A concussion is the mildest form of traumatic brain injury, and it can be caused by a blow to the head or the body. A blow causes the brain to move within the skull, which results in altered brain function. The adult human brain weighs about three pounds, is relatively soft and is surrounded by fluid. Medical experts say that a common myth is that a boxer has to be knocked out to get a concussion. In fact, over 90 percent of concussions occur without boxers being knocked out.

The consequences of a concussion are serious but typically not life-threatening. This is true when a concussion is recognized and treated, and given sufficient time to heal. According to the CDC, the symptoms of a concussion may last for days or even months.

Here is some additional data from the CDC:

—Those who have had a concussion in the past are also at risk of having another one and may find that it takes longer to recover if they have another concussion.

—Although most people recover after a concussion, how quickly they improve depends on many factors.

—Factors include how severe their concussion was, their age, how healthy they were before the concussion, and how they take care of themselves after the injury.

Experts on the subject say that about 95 percent of people who suffer a concussion recover completely. Death is rare, usually occurring only in persons who suffer a second head injury before healing from the first concussion.

Below is a Concussion Signs Symptoms Checklist and a list of Danger Signs prepared by the CDC.

A concussion can be recognized by the following signs and symptoms:

SIGNS

- Vacant stare

- Delayed verbal and motor responses

- Confusion and inability to focus attention

- Disorientation

- Slurred or incoherent speech

- Gross observable lack of coordination

- Emotions out of proportion to circumstances

- Memory deficits

- Any period of loss of consciousness

SYMPTOMS

Early (within minutes or hours)

• Headache

• Dizziness or vertigo

• Lack of awareness of surroundings

• Nausea or vomiting

Late (days to weeks later)

• Persistent low grade headache

• Lightheadedness

• Poor attention and concentration

• Memory dysfunction

• Easily fatigue

• Irritability and low frustration tolerance

• Intolerance of bright lights or difficulty focusing vision

• Intolerance of loud noises; sometimes ringing in the ears

• Anxiety and/or depressed mood

• Sleep disturbance

8

THE HISTORY
OF OPEN SCORING

The promoters of boxing matches reside in the middle class of our society while the boxers are members of the lower class, with no hope of ever slipping up in the social ladder.

The boxing system, which has been in place for 40 years, is formed by a group of people who travel around the world promoting world title boxing matches. A great percentage of the world countries are nations with a two class society: The very rich and the very poor. As such, when the system travels to such countries they are treated like royalty. They experience the life of the very wealthy. With that in mind, some of these persons lose track of reality. I know one individual who travels with two suitcases, one of them filled with pairs of shoes that cost one thousand dollars each.

This boxing domain is guarded with such zeal that change is viewed as a great threat to this existence of grandeur. The entire system rebels in anger and outrage when change is suggested. As such, the resistance to change has shackled and clouded our ability to recognize the key to progress. The system is frosted with apathy and complacency, and therefore, is in danger of an implosion.

Boxing is the only professional sport in the entertainment business which is not wealthy. The blind side of those in this business do not understand that when boxers get wealthy, their own life style also improves. A boxer is a professional that should be able to dedicate his life to improving his skills and physical condition on a daily basis. Instead, he has to work eight hours a day to earn a living.

Change is coming with or without our help. We need to implement change, which will increase the receipts at the gate. The system needs to understand that if we participate in the change process we will *not* lose control. However, if someone else makes the change we will be stuck with changes that we don't like. Boxing is the only sport that has never experienced rule changes. In basketball, football and baseball, a rule-change system is in place, which constantly writes and re-writes the rules.

During the progress of a contest, openness is paramount. All competitive sports keep the fans fully informed of the progress or the edge during the contest. Secrecy or concealment of the score gives the appearance of collusion or something dishonest. Therefore, the official score of a boxing fight must be announced at the end of every round.

The Expose It Three-Point Must

The expose it three-point-must is a system for scoring boxing. This system does not change or alter the boxing rules in any way. This history consists of a *minor administrative change* which has been tried in Arizona, and was approved by the boxing fans, proving to be superior to the existing systems. It has also turned judging into an honorable profession.

In the traditional ten-point must system the first six numbers are never used. In contrast, in the three-point must we utilize only those points being used at the present time; four numbers: zero to three. We also announce the official score during the rest period, or at the beginning of the preceding round. In order to do this, the resting period was extended from one minute to minute and a half, but modern electronic scoring technology can maintain the one-minute period.

Following is an article I wrote in 1966 regarding the state of boxing then, and my proposed changes to the system:

"Boxing is plagued by two things: First, at the end of every contest, the losing corner always protests bitterly that they were robbed because they always think that they are leading on points. Secondly, as a referee, I have observed many times the seconds in a corner lose a battle for their fighter by telling him to ease up because they thought that he was way ahead on points. And as a result have put on a dull fight.

"I hereby recommend to the State Athletic Commission that you adopt the following recommendations. These recommendations will be a big shot in the arm to the sport of boxing. And will also put the state of Arizona on the map as a progressive state in the sport of boxing. I think that you will agree that the following ideas have a world of potential.

"To remedy these conditions I recommend that the scores of the judges and the referee be collected at the end of every round, that the scores be added together and announced over the loud speaker before the start of the next round. This way the fighters know at the end of every round exactly where they stand, and won't be thinking otherwise.

"This system could turn a very close fight into one heck of a battle by incenting the guy behind to fight harder. This competitive principle is the core of most other sports, basketball, baseball, and football, and most others. You will agree that this concept is missing entirely in boxing. This system should eliminate the bitter protests that are so ever present at the end of every contest. It would revolutionize the sport to the point when the fans would no longer ask, "Who is fighting tonight?" They would say, "Let's go to the fights tonight," and that's all they would say because they would know that they would see a battle regardless of who is fighting. Nowadays one can pay to see a fight card and not see an actual fight.

"Once in a while a new judge that has little judging experience will give to a contestant say five or six points only throughout the contest, thereby creating quite a spread on points when compared with the other scorecards.

"Under the ten-point-must system of scoring one never sees less than seven points awarded to a contestant in every round. Therefore, these first seven points are superfluous.

"I further recommend that Arizona adopt the three-point-must system of scoring. The three-point-must system would avoid this condition by letting the judges know right

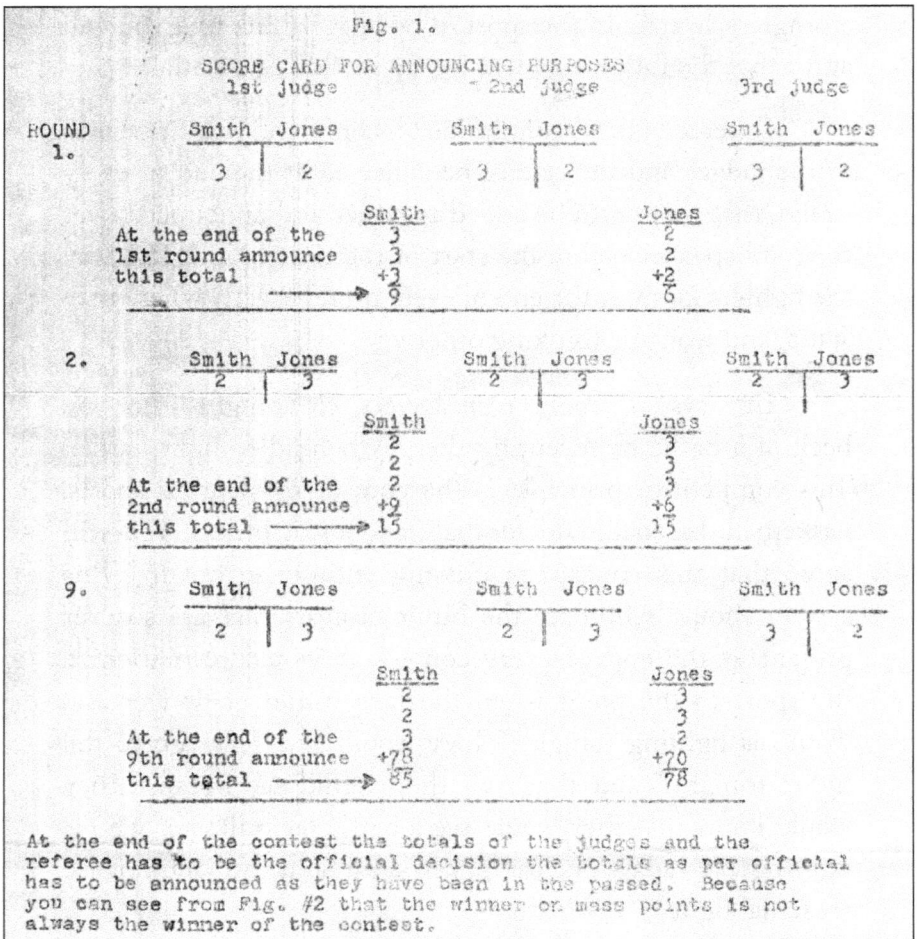

Fig. 1.

SCORE CARD FOR ANNOUNCING PURPOSES

	1st judge	2nd judge	3rd judge
	Smith Jones	Smith Jones	Smith Jones
ROUND 1.	3 | 2	3 | 2	3 | 2

At the end of the 1st round announce this total ———▶

Smith
3
3
+3
9

Jones
2
2
+2
6

2.	Smith Jones	Smith Jones	Smith Jones
	2 | 3	2 | 3	2 | 3

At the end of the 2nd round announce this total ———▶

Smith
2
2
2
+9
15

Jones
3
3
3
+6
15

9.	Smith Jones	Smith Jones	Smith Jones
	2 | 3	2 | 3	3 | 2

At the end of the 9th round announce this total ———▶

Smith
2
2
3
+78
85

Jones
3
3
2
+70
78

At the end of the contest the totals of the judges and the referee has to be the official decision the totals as per official has to be announced as they have been in the passed. Because you can see from Fig. #2 that the winner on mass points is not always the winner of the contest.

off the bat how many points they have to work with. And even a new judge would fall right into step. This system will also make the arithmetic easier in the new system of scoring.

"Figures one and two are examples of the official scoring for the proposed system.

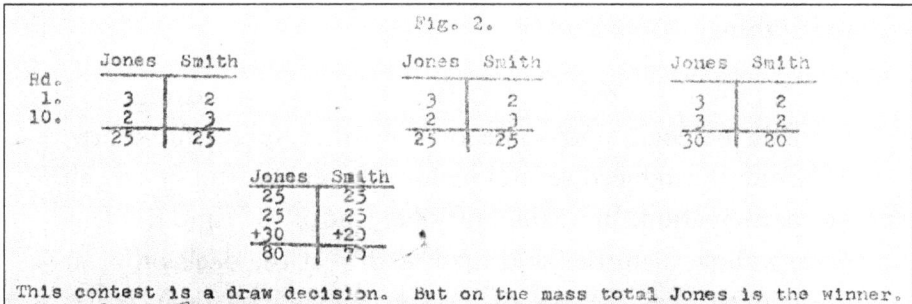

Fig. 2.

Rd.	Jones	Smith		Jones	Smith		Jones	Smith
1.	3	2		3	2		3	2
10.	2	3		2	3		3	2
	25	25		25	25		30	20

	Jones	Smith
	25	25
	25	25
	+30	+20
	80	70

This contest is a draw decision. But on the mass total Jones is the winner.

"At the end of the contest, the totals of the judges and the referee have to be the official decision. The totals as per official have to be announced as they have been passed. Because as you can see from Figure 2 that the winner on mass points is not always the winner of the contest.

"This contest is a draw decision. But on the mass total Jones is the winner."

HERE IS ANOTHER ARTICLE I WROTE IN 1968:

"The World of Boxing in 1968"

"Any World Almanac shows the rapid deterioration that the sport of boxing has experienced at the gates since it was first conceived. The meager attendances that boxing is attracting in New York City is proof enough. In the September issue of The Ring magazine one will find these attendance figures: 784, 694, 800 and 807. These are figures from one of the largest cities in the world.

"About three years ago I told myself that if boxing continued deteriorating, within five years professional boxing would be a defunct sport. Since I was not ready to accept the inevitable I asked myself if I was going to do anything about it. Odd as it may seem, in order to solve a problem one has to know what the problem is. So I set out asking... all. Everybody knew what the problem was but no two reasons were the same. Therefore one can conclude that it must be a combination of many things.

"I then started a comparison between boxing and football, baseball, and some of the other successful sports. My studies produced several major differences. The first I call fan participation. In boxing, fifty percent of the time the fans leave a show disturbed and mad. Either at the decision or at the contest itself. In any of the sports, baseball for instance, the fans leave well satisfied whether they won or lost. They leave the show discussing the merits of the game because fans go to the game to emit energy, and they do this by becoming a part of the program. They will jump up and down and have a good time. In boxing the fans don't have that opportunity because many fights are dance contests, and the score is often a mystery and a disappointment.

"Secondly, one never hears of the boxer that got his second wind. One hears about the fighter that ran out of gas and as a result got the tar knocked out of him. A boxer, because of his conditioning methods and the nature of the sport, is one of the best athletes on two feet. Therefore, one can conclude that the second wind must be of mental origin. There has to be a motivating drive to bring about the second wind.

"Thirdly, the fighters' seconds always believes that they are ahead. On numerous occasions I have seen a fight lost when the second told his fighter to take it easy because he was way ahead on points. This happens because the human mind can concentrate on only one thing at a time. They are always watching their own fighter's performance and often don't see what their opponent is doing.

"In order to get rid of these differences, I concluded that the scoring methods for boxing would have to compare with the scoring of the other sports. So I revised the present scoring methods and stipulated that the scores would have to be announced at the end of every round, thereby creating a true point system where one point can determine a winner just as is the case in all the other sports.

"The Yanez System of Scoring consists of the three-point-must and announcing the score after each round. The three-point-must system is the same as the other systems that are now in use, except that in the three-point-must I have omitted all the superfluous points because all the other systems that are now in use have a few points that are never used. For example: In the ten-point must system both contestants begin the round with ten points each. If the round is scored even, both contestants get ten points each. If the round is not even the loser gets a portion thereunder. Generally, the loser gets nine points, if he goes down once he gets eight points, if he goes down more than once and is kicked and dragged all over the ring he gets seven. But never under seven. Why then do we need the first six numbers? The five-point-must is the same but the first two numbers are never used. In the three-point-must we use four numbers: zero to three. Two judges and the referee are used to score the contest. At the end of each round the referee collects the scorecards and hands them to the commission representative at the ring side. The scores are tallied and the announcer announces the score over the loud speaker. As an example, let's say that all three scores are identical at the end of the first round and all in favor of the same fighter. Then each had three for Smith and two for Jones. The announcer would state that at the end of the first round

Smith had nine and Jones had six. The scoring then continues cumulatively. If the second round is identical to the first round, Smith would get nine additional points and Jones will get six more, for a total of eighteen and twelve respectively at the end of the second round. At the end of the contest the cumulative scores of all the Judges are announced for the final decision.

"In 1966 I introduced these changes to the State Boxing Commission and I recommended that they be tried on a trial basis. The Commission recognized the potential of these changes but they wanted opinions first, so they copied my letter and sent it to everybody in the state that was associated with boxing, and they asked for their opinions. The Yanez System promptly hit the deck. The answers were a flat NO, it just won't work. I was flabbergasted because my motives were purely altruistic. I had expected a flow of contributing hands all working for a mutual cause, the survival of boxing. However, all was not dismal, because the nays were all for different reasons.

"At this stage two of the commissioners were still in favor of further discussions because they were sure that nothing we did could hurt the sport.

"During the following year many discussions on the subject occurred. The opposition gradually submitted. My basic argument was the fact that the same people have controlled boxing for the past few decades and they have contributed nothing.

"After many discussions the Commission decided to try it out. They put the Yanez System on a trial basis. In order to give it a good trial they decided to use it on three different cards in the preliminary fights only. Piloted by the former Executive Secretary Manuel "Lito" Pena Jr., the mechanics of the scoring cards were set up and the trial period began.

"We were criticized by The Ring magazine and Sports Illustrated; they stated that we didn't need change, that we just needed better officials.

"During the trial period the system proved itself on every count at least once. During one four rounder, one of the contestants lead by one point on the first three rounds, and on the last round the other contestant came on so strong that the first contestant lost the fight by one point. The losing fighter grabbed the mic and protested that he had won the first three rounds therefore he should have won the contest. This fighter learned that in the new system one can never let up; he has to fight to the last minute. In several fights the score jumped back and forth with a lot of fighting in between. During the trial period it was obvious to all that fighters don't give up. On several occasions a contestant that was way behind at the closing rounds would flurry, get his second wind, and KO his opponent.

"Very often one will hear that name fighters are the answer. The Moore vs. Fullmer fight is a good example that this is not the case, had it not been for the new scoring system these two fighters would have been booed right out of the ring because it was one of the worst fights that we had seen in a long time. The attached article dated February 21, 1968 shows that the fight was scored very close, and as a result a state of excitement prevailed for the duration of the fight. Deep silence would prevail just prior to the announcement of the score. The arena atmosphere resembled the basketball gymnasium where all cheer and yell. The dissension that prevails at the end of many fights also disappeared.

"Even the judging segment of the game changed; it became an honorable one because the fans were developing confidence in them. The system of three judges is a very good one because judges are human and they are also boxing fans, therefore it is very easy for one of them to be partial to one of the contestants. When that happens the other two will check him.

"When the system had been in use for some time I asked a fighter if he liked the new system, and he said that he didn't like it because he had to fight harder. The commission made some hand-outs with which to check fan opinion. On the third card the hand-outs that came back were to the tune of 83 percent in favor of the new system. The announcer also asked the fans for a verbal vote which was also overwhelmingly approved.

"At the end of the trial period the commission did not hesitate to adopt the new system. Commissioner Mike Quihuis stated that the will of the people could not be ignored. So on December 20, 1967, Commission Chairman Bill Warren, Dr. Robert Shannon, and Mike Quihuis formally adopted the new system as the Arizona way of scoring boxing contests. Also present at that meeting was Al Fenn who also endorsed the new system.

"In 1967, the year closed with two fights that drew 300 fans. The Yanez System went into effect on January 1968, and the first four boxing matches drew more than 1,000 fans each. It had been ten years since we had seen that kind of consistent attendance. This proved that good hard fighting is what the people want, regardless of who is fighting. Arizona boxer Tony Anchondo (4-15) is a good example. He was one of the worst fighters that has ever stepped into the ring but the fans loved him. He would fight a bear if you put one in the ring.

"In 1968, after four shows the new Commission Chairman Dr. Robert Shannon and Mr. Jay Edson, who had just returned into town, suspended the new system until the mechanics of the arithmetic could be reworked. The day before the next fight, the newspaper announced that the new system would no longer be used, that the ten-point-must would be used. That fight, Don Fullmer vs. Billy Marsh, on April 25, 1968 should have drawn 1,500 fans; it drew 700. The following fight, Tony Doyle vs. Chris Jones attracted 500 fans. It appears that the advent of the TV set saved us. In summary, the Yanez System did everything that we had hoped it would do and then some. It instilled fan participation and made the fighters fight harder. Even the second wind emerged.

"In approximately 1970, Vince Leary and I promoted amateur boxing matches at Magoo's on 19th Avenue and Van Buren, every two weeks for several months. We had 15 to 20 fights per show. A donation was the price for admission. All monies collected were used to buy trophies for the kids.

"We used the three-point-must for scoring and I was the referee. No judges were used. I announced the score after each round. Every single fight was a drag-out affair. Several hundred fights and 99 percent were good fights. We had no complaints from the fans or the fighters for the entire duration. The kids would line up at the back door of the club, and Al Fenn would match them up. We had to stop promoting because the bar was too small and it became overwhelmed with too many kids."

I should add that during the trial period of the three-point must, we had three shows. In each card we used the new system in the preliminary fights. The main event was still scored with the 10-point must system. And we announced the official score at the end of every round. The Boxing Commission felt that we would need more time for the scorekeeper, so they added half a minute to the rest of the period between rounds. In the existing scoring system, number nine and ten were the most used. In the new system the most used numbers are two and three. Therefore, by the second show, the half minute that was added to the rest of the period was dropped, as not needed. A few things changed in 1967, since it was election year: The Executive Director, Manuel Pena Jr. was elected to the State Legislature, so he had to resign as the director of boxing. One commissioner left, so Dr. Shannon became the new Chair for the Boxing Commission.

In 1968, after four boxing shows with the three-point-must system in place, Dr. Shannon arbitrarily unilaterally, without approval from the other commissioners, dropped the system, and stopped announcing the score at the end of each round. In his letter[1] he stated there were mechanical operational problems that needed to be resolved. Since the only thing that we changed was the numbering system, that went from using the number ten and nine to three and two, I concluded that he had *no* intelligent reason for dropping the three-point must.

OPEN SCORING IN THE MEDIA

In June 1967, the *Arizona Republic* published a short notice about a meeting where the Arizona Athletic Commission was scheduled to discuss a revised boxing scoring system. The notice mentions my name as the proponent of a "3-point must scoring system and abolishment of the current 10-point must system for state boxing matches. Yanez also will ask that officials' scorecards be read at the end of each round." (Sports Briefly. 1967, June 9. Ring Revision Sought. The *Arizona Republic*).

In July 1967, the *Arizona Republic* published a short article about a boxing match where the new scoring system was going to be tried for the first time. The piece mentions that State Athletic Commission chairman William Warren had a meeting with all state boxing officials to explain the new system. The system is described in the article as a "three-point must system" with the two Judges and referee's score-cards to be collected and totaled at the end of each round. "In effect, the system will eliminate split decisions. Also, instead of one-minute

---

1   See page 65 for scan of original letter and page 108 for transcript.

rest periods between rounds, competitors will be given 1½ minutes," the article adds. (1967, July 26. Bout Tomorrow Tests New Scoring System. The *Arizona Republic*).

The *Phoenix Gazette* recorded the first time the open scoring system was used. In the December 20, 1967 edition, reporter Tim Tyers describes the use of the system during the Manny Elias vs. Raul Carreon fight at the Phoenix Madison Square Garden arena. "A sparse crowd of 300 (an optimistic estimate) saw the fight. It was also the first fight held under the three-point must system, the state's newly adopted scoring's system." Tyers adds that during this fight, "each judge gave three points to the winner of a round, and two or less to the loser. Each scorecard was added at the end of the round and announced over the public address system." (Tyers, T. 1967, December 20. Elias Holds State Title; Foe Rugged. The *Phoenix Gazette*).

In the December 25, 1967 edition of *Sports Illustrated*, in the "Scorecard" section, the magazine called my proposed scoring system "pointless," after its implementation. The piece was written after the Arizona Athletic Commission announced point scores at boxing fights in the state after each round. *Sports Illustrated* pointed out in criticism that "the commission should have changed its Judges instead of the rules." Because the traditional minute-long time-out between each round was being extended to a minute and a half to allow officials enough time to collect and announce their scoring after each round, the magazine felt the boxer who would be in a better condition during a fight was going to be "penalized," apparently because the other boxer will have some extra time to recover. The publication also thought that since this change was only applicable in Arizona, that "local fighters who become accustomed to the longer rest will be affected adversely when boxing out of state." Moreover, *Sports Illustrated* criticized Arizona judges calling them "weak," and saying that under the new system they could be undoubtedly "influenced by booing if highly partisan fans should disagree with their scoring." The sports publication summarized its dislike of the new scoring system by stating: "Forget it, Arizona." ("Scorecard". 1967, December 25. *Sports Illustrated*).

The *Gazette* also mentioned the three-point system in a sports note in the February 21, 1968 edition of the paper, written again by reporter Tim Tyers, who quotes Utah boxer Don Fullmer saying: "I thought I had him [rival Phoenix boxer Carl Moore] by at least three points going into the eighth... When they announced it was 75-75 after the ninth, I was worried. I knew if Moore has just one good flurry in the tenth, they would give him the fight." Apparently, the fact that Fullmer was aware of the score *prior* to the end of the bout made him push harder and eventually defeat Moore. This is in fact one of the benefits I mention about the open scoring system. (Tyers, T. 1968, February 21. Fullmer Voted Ring Victory; Carl Close. The *Phoenix Gazette*).

I mentioned that the commission surveyed fans through a printed handout distributed at the fights so they could express their like or dislike of the new scoring system. The text read as follows:

"Dear Boxing Fan:

"By public request, we will use a new method of scoring tonight, and are requesting your opinion of this system.

"In brief, this new system, which will be used for the UNDER-CARD bouts only, consists of three changes as follows: (1) Scoring will be based on 0 to 3 points. (2) In-between-rounds rest period will be 1½ minute. (3) Scores will be announced at the end of each round. The boxer with the highest sum total at the end of the bout, as in the past, will be declared the winner.

"To help us to further determine the merits of this new scoring system, we request your cooperation. Please note your opinion, in the area shown on this card, and deposit this in one of the large boxes located at each exit.

"Thank you,

ARIZONA ATHLETIC COMMISSION

X   Yes----I like this new scoring system.

O   No----I do not like this new scoring system."

LETTERS

January 23, 1967

Arizona State Athletic Commission
823 West Adams
Phoenix, Arizona 85007

Attention: William Warren, Chairman

Dear Bill:

I have given quite a bit of thought to the proposed Three Point Must scoring system advocated by Referee Roger Yanez. Roger is to be complimented and commended for the thought he has given this matter and the time expended outlining the method of scoring.

I should like however to go on record as being opposed to the proposed scoring system. First of all, such a system is not used by any Boxing Commission in the world. This is true possibly for some of the following reasons:

1. Scorecards are now added and checked at the end of each fight. Even then occasionally error creeps in. If said scorecards were gathered and added at the end of each round, you multiply the possibility of error by the number of rounds of the fight. In other words, in a ten round fight there are ten times as many chances for error, and in a fifteen round fight fifteen times as many chances for error as under the present system.

2. Roger points out that sometimes a new judge lacking experience does not see the fight as do the more experienced judges. If on the illustration, Judge 3, referred to as the third

judge of the Smith-Jones fight, is the new judge, then his error is magnified and Jones would be the winner of the fight by a considerable margin in spite of the fact that two out of three, and at that the two more experienced judges, saw the fight a draw.

3. On the other hand, a judge sitting in his particular spot, and seeing the fight from his angle, hearing the scores at the end of each round, and realizing that his scoring was, some if not vastly, different from the other judges, might be influenced by the other judges' decision. This would in turn eliminate the very purpose or reason for which judges sit on different sides of the ring.

These are the three principal defects to the proposed new scoring system which come immediately to my mind. Undoubtedly, there are others. I trust that my comments will be of some aid in helping the members of the Commission arrive at a decision.

Thank you.

Sincerely,

STEPHEN W. CONNORS

SWC:bl

cc: T. R. Mofford

      Mike Quihuis

April 7, 1967
State Athletic Commission
823 W. Adams

Dear Chairman Warren:

Roger Yanez talked to me about a change that he has proposed, to the Commission, for scoring of boxing.

I strongly recommend that the commission adopt this change, for I have seen it work. In 1956 I had a fight in Florida where a system similar to this one was used.

The score was being posted after each round. At the end of the 4th round I was very sure that I was way ahead when my second told me that I was behind. The score was three to one. My second then told me that I could only win by a knockout. I then went after him and knocked him out. If I had not known the score at the end of the 4th round I might have lost that fight.

At the end of that fight the audience really applauded. I am sure they were applauding only the 5th round because I stopped some good ones myself while going for the knockout.

Respectfully yours,

Alex M. Fimbrez

Mr. Roger Yanez
1624 W. Chipman Rd
Phoenix, Arizona 85041

Dear Roger:

In reply to your recent letter requesting the status of your three point must scoring system by this Commission, please be advised that this scoring method is in a state of inactivity since we are still awaiting further elements of clarification from you concerning your recommendations for improving the mechanical operation of this system.

I again state that this scoring system of yours does have merit, but there are many weak points in its physical operation. When you feel you have the corrective measures made that will afford its use, please bring these recommendations to the attention of this Commission, in writing. Upon this receipt, I assure you that your scoring system, with its recommendations will be most seriously considered by me personally, as well as by the entire Commission.

Assuming that your recommendations will place this scoring system before the Commission in its final form, after due consideration, study, and deliberation, this Commission will then vote upon the acceptance or rejection of this new scoring system.

My kind regards are enclosed to you and yours.

Sincerely,

R. K. SHANNON, Chairman

RKS:gb

9

THE ASSOCIATION
OF BOXING COMMISSIONS
The International Professional Ring Officials
and the Muhammad Ali Act

The Association of Boxing Commissions (ABC), the International Professional Ring Officials (IPRO), and the Muhammad Ali Boxing Reform Act are the only meaningful things that have happened to boxing in the United States in the last one hundred years.

The ABC was formed in the 1980s when various executive directors of a number of boxing commissions met to discuss how boxing was handled in their respective jurisdictions. The ABC aims to:

-Promote uniform health and safety standards in boxing and MMA;

-Provide accurate records for boxers and mixed martial artists;

-Increase communication between organizations;

-Publish medical and training information and education for all boxing and MMA related professionals;

-Establish and ran a charitable foundation to aid indigent boxers;

-Encourage adherence to, and enforcement of, applicable federal laws by each member of the ABC;

-Retain Fight Fax Record book as the Official record keeper for results of professional boxing.

The IPRO was organized by Barry Druxman—a licensed referee and judge for the State of Washington—to gather a meeting of the minds of those officials who care about the sport of boxing. Druxman acted after recognizing the need for greater training and dialogue among world-rated boxing officials.

It appears that the boxing world has a brain that has been frozen for a long time. The only minor changes that have occurred are in the scoring methods. A few years ago, the state of New York used the round system of scoring, and the rest of the country was using the five-point system. Sometime later everybody just turned to the ten-point system. For some reason or another they have never noticed that the numbers zero through six are never used, so why do we need them?

The Muhammad Ali Boxing Reform Act, enacted in 2000 and sponsored by Michael Oxley, representative from Ohio, amended the Professional Safety Act of 1996. The Ali Act seems to be an important legislation that brought change to boxing. In various occasions, Arizona Senator John McCain—an avid boxing fan—told me that he was working to support this act. The purposes of this Act are:

(1) to protect the rights and welfare of professional boxers on an interstate basis by preventing certain exploitive, oppressive, and unethical business practices;

(2) to assist State boxing commissions in their efforts to provide more effective public oversight of the sport;

(3) to promote honorable competition in professional boxing and enhance the overall integrity of the industry.

This Act amends the 1996 Professional Boxing Safety Act by expanding upon legislature against exploitation, conflict of interest, enforcement, and as well as additional amendments.

This is a very beautiful Act since it includes all the do's and don'ts that already exist in other professional sports, but the ABC and the USBA don't understand that these rules are meaningless unless we are in front of a judge, and we will never get to talk to one until we get 20 thousand fans at all of our club fights.

10

THE TELEVISION ANALYST

When I watch a boxing match on the television, I always set the volume knob in the off position. Which means that the fight experts have been a significant part of what caused the demise of professional boxing or at best they have branded the boxing judge as an incompetent sort.

The eternal barrage of meaningless negative rhetoric from the boxing commentators is in constant conflict with the action in the ring. Often, it appears that the expert is not viewing the same match as the judges.

The expert is not aware that every boxer that is in the ring has a mama that is watching the fight. He has not learned that dwelling on negatives is not a good thing, that every fighter has attributes that have earned him the right to be in the ring. The mere fact that he has the courage to climb into the ring indicates that he is a very brave person. In other words: if you can't think of attributes that a boxer might possess, it would be best for them to remain silent. On the golf course, fans are told to remain silent when the golfer is getting ready to swing his club.

The fight analyst has never noticed that he is wrong more often than not, or has never considered that as the boxing expert, he should never be wrong, or at least not as often.

The UniMás Channel (formerly Telefutura) is the only channel that has analysts that do not malign the warriors, and admit it when they are wrong. So maybe it's a cultural thing? UniMás is an American Spanish-language broadcast television network owned by Univision Communications.

By using the open scoring method, those experts can sit behind the scoring tables and therein get a different perspective of the fights.

11

THE UNITED STATES BOXING ADMINISTRATION
(USBA)

Officially, the United States Boxing Administration (USBA) was established under the Professional Boxing Amendments Act of 2002 to protect the health, safety, and general interests of boxers. Among other things, the amendment required an Indian tribe to establish a boxing commission to regulate professional boxing matches held on its reservation, and prohibits a person from arranging, promoting, or fighting in a match in a State or Indian land unless the match is approved by the USBA, established under this Act, and supervised by a boxing commission that is a member of the Association of Boxing Commissions.

Historically, places without those rules and regulations would hire a State that has a boxing commission to supervise their shows. In 14 years, the USBA has managed to create an enormous amount of prose and paperwork. The USBA states that: "The law stipulates that the States boxing commissions would retain all of the powers, duties and functions as long as they were not inconsistent with the federal law." Forget the fact that the boxing states have regulated the sport for 297 years, since 1719. The reason that the States: "Would retain their powers and duties," it's a short sentence in Article 10 of the United States Constitution, which states that the government cannot usurp State Constitutions. Therefore, the USBA should not create minimum standards because existing *essential* rules are already in place in several states, where the fan base is so low that the promoters cannot afford the venue's rent.

In the last 14 years, the USBA has built a pyramid in the middle of the Sahara Desert, so now I wonder who is going to enjoy the fruits of their majestic temple; a temple of prose and paperwork that is in a desert absent of the nomads. The USBA is wandering around, lost in a dense forest, like the dog that is chasing his own tail. The ABC has not noticed that the remaining boxing fans are located in Las Vegas, and that they are highly upset. Now they created what they call "minimum standards," for the purpose of replacing what is highly essential, rules which were developed over a period of 297 years.

It now appears that John McCain, United States Senator for Arizona, noticed the absence of the boxing fans in the arenas, so he added to the Ali Act a decree that it would be "self-funded." However, it appears that no one noticed that we are a sport without boxing fans.

All of these rules and regulations are supposed to be for the benefit of the boxers, the persons who live in the very low-level of our financial system, which means that the gladiators are very poor folks. In a world where 99 percent of those in professional sports are wealthy. Therefore, we can rightly conclude that the Muhammad Ali Act was created to help extricate the professional boxer. So the question arises: Do we give the ABC and the USBA twenty additional years to help, or do we not?

I restate that in 1950 the population of Phoenix was 50,000. Today it is 4.3 million, approximately 860 percent larger. In 1950, the fan base was 300. To this day the fan base has not increased arith-metically.

The USBA has existed for 14 years, and how has it helped our fighters? Fighters who have to work for a living. Maybe we should ask Senator McCain to pasteurize the ABC, to the thinking fields, until they realize that we are all here for the purpose of elevating the statures of our warriors. Put the ABC in a pasture, with a two-year limit; if they don't produce let them just fade away because another 14 years to help the sport of boxing is excessive.

At this time I will not restate Einstein's theory regarding meaning-less repetition. I will merely state that the ABC is ill-informed, because they are not aware of their intended goals or mission. So please do not tell me that professional boxing is safer because pro boxing is one of the safest sports in town. An attribute of the Ali Act is that it is self-funded, therefore the ABC is able to write-off expenses as entertainment. In Arizona, progress has been in the wrong direction. In 2015 and 2016, I paid $30 for a ticket to watch a professional fight where I saw mostly amateur fights. The boxing fans were appeased with noise in the range of 120 decibels and lighting of many colors, all night.

It now appears that the Arizona Boxing Commission does not know the difference between professional boxing and amateur boxing. Therefore, I now recommend that the method of open scoring be implemented. My experience indicates that the revenues will instantly increase, one thousand percent, and continue to grow geometrically.

This professional boxing *stubbornness* (quagmire) that is drowning the sport of boxing must be corrected. The August 2016 issue of The Ring magazine shows that we have 17 different weight divisions in professional boxing, and that the U.S. does *not* have one single world champion in any of those divisions. Therefore, we can conclude that the sport of boxing is a worldwide sport.

My personal diary shows that in December 20, 1967, the Arizona Boxing Commission adopted the Yanez Three-Point System of scoring Professional Boxing. At that meeting, Commissioner Quihuis stated that he seconded the motion to adopt the new system because the boxing fans voted to endorse the system by 83 percent, therefore that the "will" of the people could not be ignored. The diary also shows that in 1968, the new Chairman of the Boxing Commission, Dr. Shannon, unilaterally arbitrarily stopped the use of the Three-Point-Must System of Scoring Boxing in Arizona. Therefore, it is still the Law in Arizona.

In reviewing the ABC's rules dated January 25, 2006, I find that 50 percent of those rules are *not* acceptable. The ABC has failed to notice that the rules and the atmosphere in professional boxing are not similar to those of other professional sports. In their training sessions for boxing officials, they state that a score of less than 70 percent is a failed test, which means that a certain percentage of their students wasted their time attending class, and due to poor instruction by an instructor who did not know how to teach, students are branded as dummies. In my classes, a score of excellence was the only score that was acceptable; no one could leave the classroom until they had mastered the subject or understood what the instructor was trying to teach.

I now suggest to the boxing fans that if you agree with this proposal, that you contact the Governor of Arizona or call him, requesting that he directs his Boxing Commission to follow the existing law, which was adopted in 1967 by that Boxing Commission. It used the Yanez Open Scoring System for professional boxing in Arizona.

Governor Doug Ducey
1700 West Washington Street Phoenix, AZ 85007
(602-542-4331)
www.azgovernor.gov

Boxing fans elsewhere in the U.S. call your own boxing or athletic commission that regulates this sport. Please don't wait for Arizona to clean it up, because we blew it once already.

12

EXAMINATION FOR BOXING REFEREES AND JUDGES

1. (T) (F) A boxing ring should have four ropes.

2. (T) (F) The referee should examine gloves before a contest. If the gloves are found to be excessively worn or unsanitary, he can request that they be changed.

3. (T) (F) Gloves for all main events shall be new.

4. (T) (F) All clubs shall have on hand two extra sets of gloves in case gloves in use are damaged or need to be replaced.

5. (T) (F) Six-ounce gloves may be used only in championship bouts.

6. (T) (F) The maximum amount of surgeon's tape and bandages for use on each hand is two feet and ten yards respectively.

7. (T) (F) The referee does not have the authority to remove excessive grease or foreign substance from a contestant's face.

8. (T) (F) Abdominal guards are optional during boxing contests.

9. (T) (F) Any boxer guilty of deliberate foul tactics in a contest can be disqualified by the referee.

10. (T) (F) The disposition of the purse and boxing license of a boxer who has been disqualified for foul tactics during a contest is up to the referee.

11. (T) (F) If a boxer's chances have not been jeopardized as a result of an accidental foul, the referee may order the bout to continue after a reasonable interval.

12. (T) (F) Seconds are held strictly responsible for the enforcement of practices likely to cause injury to the contestants.

13. (T) (F) The only fair blow is a blow delivered with the padded knuckle part of the glove, on the front or side of the head and above the belt.

14. (T) (F) The referee does not have the power to deduct points from a fighter if he has been warned against minor fouls such as wrestling or holding.

15. (T) (F) The referee should make an effort to steal the show by repeatedly separating the fighters, even if not necessary.

16. (T) (F) The referee has the power to stop a contest if he considers it to be one sided or if either contestant is in such condition that to continue might subject him to serious injury.

17. (T) (F) In case of an injury to one of the contestants the referee has to call into the ring the club physician for examination of the injured contestant before rendering a decision.

18. (T) (F) If the referee decides that the contestants are not seriously or honestly competing, that the knockdown is a dive, he shall not finish the knockdown count but shall stop the fight and order the purses of both boxers held pending investigation by the commission. And announce that no decision has been rendered.

19. (T) (F) A referee may not penalize a contestant for unintentional fouls.

20. (T) (F) The referee shall notify the judges, at the conclusion of a

round, in which he penalized a contestant for fouling as to the number of points to be deducted from a contestant.

21. (T) (F) No contestant can be awarded a contest on a claim of a low blow foul.

22. (T) (F) On a claim of a low blow foul a "no decision contest" shall be rendered by the referee.

23. (T) (F) If an accidental butt occurs during the first round, in which a contestant is incapacitated, the fight will be called a draw by the referee.

24. (T) (F) If a boxer is accidentally butted so that he cannot continue, the referee shall call the bout a technical draw if the injured boxer is behind on points or declare the injured boxer the winner on a technical decision if he has a lead on points.

25. (T) (F) If a contestant does not answer the bell the referee shall award a TKO decision to his opponent as of the round that is coming up.

26. (T) (F) When a contestant's gloves touch the floor they pickup foreign particles, therefore it's the referees duty to wipe the gloves.

27. (T) (F) During a knockdown, the timekeeper's count is the official count.

28. (T) (F) During a knockdown, the referee should announce the passing of the seconds softly so that he is the only one that knows what is going on.

29. (T) (F) During a knockdown the referee should follow the second intervals as they are being announced by the timekeeper.

30. (T) (F) A contestant who is knocked down has to resume boxing before the count of ten but not before the count of eight.

31. (T) (F) If a contestant does not stay in the farthest corner during a knockdown, the referee shall cease counting until he has returned to the corner.

32. (T) (F) If a boxer who is down arises during the count, the referee may, if he deems it advisable, step between the contestants long enough to assure himself that the boxer just arisen is in a fit condition to continue.

33. (T) (F) If a contestant is knocked down during the last ten seconds of a round and the bell sounds indicating the end of the round, the count shall continue the same as though the round was not ended.

34. (T) (F) If a contestant is knocked down and counted out after the end of the round, the knockout shall be considered as having taken place during the round which follows.

35. (T) (F) Should a contestant who is down arise before the count of ten is reached and go down immediately without being struck, the referee shall start the count anew.

36. (T) (F) When a boxer falls out of the ring and over the edge of the platform, the referee should allow a reasonable time for his return.

37. (T) (F) A contestant who deliberately wrestles or throws from the ring should be penalized.

38. (T) (F) The referee can count a contestant out either on the ropes or on the floor.

39. (T) (F) A contestant is deemed down when any part of his body, other than feet, touches the floor.

40. (T) (F) A contestant cannot be deemed down when still standing even though he is unable to defend himself.

41. (T) (F) At the termination of all bouts the announcer shall announce the winner, then raise his hand.

42. (T) (F) A decision rendered at the termination of any boxing contest is final and cannot be changed by the commission or anyone else.

43. (T) (F) After a fight, the commission representative may show the scorecards to the press if they so desire.

44. (T) (F) On judging a contest, not less than seven points should be given to a contestant in any one round.

45. (T) (F) On judging a contest, fractions of points may be given to a contestant when it is felt that a round was fairly even.

46. (T) (F) In case of fouls or infractions of the rules the referee shall be the sole judge of the number of points to be deducted from the offender and shall so notify the judges.

47. (T) (F) When the referee takes away a round from a contestant for a foul, he may put an asterisk(*) next to the number of the round lost on the scorecard and at the bottom of the card indicate "round lost due to foul."

48. (T) (F) When the referee takes away points from a contestant for fouling, he should so inform both contestants of the penalty at the end of the respective round.

49. (T) (F) A boxer can be penalized in a latter round by virtue of a previous foul or infraction of the rules.

50. (T) (F) A second may throw into the ring his towel to indicate that the fight be halted at any time he feels his fighter is in danger of serious injury if the fight were to continue.

51. (T) (F) A boxer who has been knocked out should be kept in a prone position until he has recovered.

52. (T) (F) Stimulants or drugs may be used during the course of a fight if they are beneficial to the fighter and if used with caution

53. (T) (F) Collodion may be used over a fighter's eyes to protect recent cuts.

54. (T) (F) Any excessive or undue spraying or throwing of water on any boxer between rounds is forbidden.

55. (T) (F) A second may toss a towel into the ring in token of the defeat of his boxer.

56. (T) (F) The use of collodion is prohibited in Paragraph 145, and is subject to disciplinary action.

57. (T) (F) Ten seconds before the beginning of each round the timekeeper will blow a warning whistle.

58. (T) (F) Judges and referees are selected by the promoters.

59. (T) (F) The commission selects all the referees with special attention for championship contests or contests considered by the commission to be special events.

60. (T) (F) The commission determines qualifications and standards for referees and judges.

61. (T) (F) No licensee can verbally or physically abuse a referee without being reprimanded.

62. (T) (F) It is recommended that a referee send a written complaint to the commission in the event that he is abused in any way by another licensee.

63. (T) (F) The commission may revoke or suspend any license granted under the provisions of the Arizona Statute, for reasons unbecoming that of a professional person.

64. (T) (F) A referee does not have to present himself, for a contest, in a clean and neat appearance.

65. (T) (F) Effective aggressiveness should always be a very important consideration in scoring a content.

66. (T) (F) It is not possible for a contestant to win a fight if he is always back peddling.

67. (T) (F) During the course of a contest, if the trunks of one of the contestants become torn to the point that he is indecent, the referee should immediately stop the fight and award it to the contestant still wearing the good trunks.

68. (T) (F) An official involved in scoring a contest or in rendering a just and honest verdict must first of all be thoroughly lacking in bias.

69. (T) (F) An official scoring a contest should pay close attention to the feelings of the audience as a guide toward accurate scoring.

70. (T) (F) An official should keep an open mind, show no prejudice, watch the action closely and render the verdict as he sees it.

71. (T) (F) Spectators not keeping score can be just as accurate in rendering a decision as the judges keeping score.

72. (T) (F) Ineffective aggressiveness should not receive the same credit as effective counter punching and clearer boxing.

73. (T) (F) Leading and missing consistently is considered effective aggressiveness.

74. (T) (F) The belt line is the imaginary line that runs from hip bone to hip bone.

75. (T) (F) If a glove should burst during the progress of a contest, the referee should stop the fight and obtain a new one.

76. (T) (F) If a lace should become loose and there is no danger, the round should be completed before the lace is tightened. But if there is danger, the referee should halt the contest and fasten the lace but take time out while doing it.

77. (T) (F) Persistent holding is not considered sufficient cause for disqualification of a boxer by the referee.

78. (T) (F) The referee should not interfere with a boxer who is attempting to strike at his opponent while the latter is holding on and the former has one hand free.

79. (T) (F) It is alright if the referee or one of the judges gives a signal to a friend as to the winner of each round, so long as no one else is aware of the signaling.

80. (T) (F) During the course of a contest, the referee should not be harsh in the treatment of the fighters by manhandling, pushing, shoving or slapping when it becomes necessary to break them from a clinch.

81. (T) (F) If a boxer's mouth piece falls to the canvas the referee should stop the fight to give the fighter a chance to replace it.

82. (T) (F) When a contestant persistently delays the action by clinching and holding, the referee should first warn the offender then deduct points if he persists.

83. (T) (F) During the progress of a contest the judges should signal to each other with a hidden signal or sign as to the winner of each round. But only in such a way that the public is not aware that the signaling is going on.

13

THE RING MAGAZINE AND THE RATING SYSTEMS

T he Ring magazine is a sports magazine that was first published in 1922 by Nat Fleischer, and is currently owned by Oscar De La Hoya's Golden Boy Enterprises, which acquired it in 2007.

The library of this magazine has a colorful and interesting history of professional boxing dating back to 1887. It includes bare-knuckles' fighting between boxers Jake Kilrain vs. John L. Sullivan in 1889 under a temperature of 106 degrees. The fight was stopped due to rain. It also includes the first fight under the Marquis of Queensberry rules in 1892 between boxers James Corbett and John L. Sullivan.

The Ring started the fighter rating system in the different weight divisions. In 1968, they had a total of eight different divisions. Over the years, several different organizations have established themselves as professional boxing authorities with their own rating systems. They rate only individuals who are due-paying members.

As a result, the many different "authorities" have numerous different champions in all the different weight divisions. The number of different divisions has grown from eight to sixteen. The more champions there are the better the hip, which means more money for everybody. The three major authorities that have survived are: the World Boxing

Council, (WBC), the International Boxing Federation (IBF), and the World Boxing Association (WBA).

For several years, The Ring magazine would publish all the different ratings in their respective different authorities, which gave everybody free advertising and legitimized their status as an authority. A few years ago, The Ring stopped including the other rating systems, probably due to a business decision.

www.ingramcontent.com/pod-product-compliance
Lightning Source LLC
Chambersburg PA
CBHW060352090426
42734CB00011B/2111